Finishing Well

FOCUSING ON THE ESSENTIALS FOR MINISTRY HEALTH

Dale M. Wolyniak

Peak Vista Press
Peyton, Colorado
www.peakvistapress.com

Finishing Well: Focusing on the Essentials for Ministry Health

© 2008 by Dale M. Wolyniak

Published by Peak Vista Press
18070 Tonto Court
Peyton, Colorado 80831
www.peakvistapress.com

Cover Design by Danielle J. Hull
Hull Design - 303.842.7202

Printed in the United States of America

All rights reserved. No part of this publication may be reproduced, stored in a retrieval system, or transmitted in any form or by any means – for example, electronic, photocopy, recording – without the prior written permission of the publisher. The only exception is brief quotations in printed reviews or educational research papers.

ISBN 978-0-9822295-2-1

Scripture quotations, unless otherwise noted, are from the HOLY BIBLE, NEW INTERNATIONAL VERSION. Copyright 1973,1978,1984 by International Bible Society. Used by permission. All rights reserved.

This book is dedicated to all those men and women
who serve faithfully
in
our Lord's vineyard.

May they find encouragement and help
in the pages of this book.

As Philippians 3:14 reads:

*"I press on toward the goal
to win the prize
for which
God has called me
heavenward
in Christ Jesus"*.

Endorsements

"It does not take a disciplined observer very long to note that any ministry -- specifically pastoral ministry -- can be hazardous to one's health. Dale, in his book, *Finishing Well*, does an excellent job of pinpointing the hazards of ministry, but goes even further to write for all of us a prescription -- that if followed -- will result in healthy life patterns. To finish well is the ultimate goal for all of us who serve the church ... are you ready for a check-up?"

- ***H.B. London, Jr.***
Vice President,
Church & Clergy, Focus on the Family

"In *'Finishing Well'*, Dale Wolyniak effectively defines the nature of ministry and its many challenges. He then offers insightful guidelines to help ministers navigate through a lifetime of work. I highly recommend this book to all my fellow ministers."

- ***Don Steiger***
Superintendent, Rocky Mountain District Council, Assemblies of God

"Dale Wolyniak's book, *"Finishing Well",* is a practical, easy-to-read book that is written by a brother who knows ministry well. Having served as a fellow pastor near him in Colorado, plus as a regional superintendent, I know Dale has learned the truths spelled out in the book from his own authentic experience as a missionary and pastor. This book contains necessary information for anyone who feels called of God to vocational ministry in the church; it will be a life of provision and grace, but also stress and difficulty…and finishing well will not be easy."

- ***G. Robert Cook, Jr.***
Executive Vice President,
The Alliance for Assemblies of God Higher Education

TABLE OF CONTENTS

ACKNOWLEDGEMENTS... i

Chapter

1. **INTRODUCTION** 1

2. **GENERAL CALL**... 7
    Defining the Theological Basis
    The General Call
    Old Testament Precedents to the Call of God
    New Testament Precedents to the Call of God
    Summary

3. **SPECIAL CALL TO MINISTRY** 15
    Old Testament Call to Leadership
    New Testament Call to Leadership
    Requirements of Leadership from the Epistles
    Contemporary Authors
    Summary

4. **TOP STRESSORS OF MINISTERS TODAY** 33
    Stress Defined
    National Survey Results on Pastoral Stress
    Who are the Most Stressed-out Pastors?
    Summary of Leadership Survey, 1997
    Summary of How Pastors Rate Survey, 2003
    Focus On the Family Pastoral Care Reports
    The Author's Survey Results
    Missionary Member Care
    Summary

5. **A THREEFOLD CORD** 57
    Character and the Minister
    Developing Competency Skills for Ministry
    Commitment and the Minister
    Summary

6. **STYLE OF LEADERSHIP**..81
    Leadership Defined
    Five Smooth Stones
    Giftedness
    Leadership Styles
    Servant Leader
    Four Styles of Relating
    Personality Type and Leadership Style
    Concept of Team Leadership
    Modeling Christ as a Leader
    The Kingdom Style of Leadership
    Mentoring as a Means of Leadership Enhancement
    Summary

7. **TIME MANAGEMENT**..99
    Evaluate How Time is Used
    Effective Planning
    Delegate Activities and Tasks to Others
    Working with a Job Description
    Practical Observations
    Summary

8. **ACCOUNTABILITY**...109
    Develop a Support Team
    Accountability as a Safeguard
    Reporting is Accountability
    Depending on Other People
    Maintenance of Healthy Habits of Accountability
    Establishing a Ministry Philosophy

9. **NURTURING RELATIONSHIPS**............................119
    A Definition of Relational Stress
    A Personal Walk With God
    Spouse and Family
    Interpersonal Relationships
    The Loneliness Factor
    Summary

10. **DEMANDS AND EXPECTATIONS**............................131
    Defining the Pastoral Role
    Developing a Pace of Living
    Delegation as a Tool for Leadership
    When Conflict Comes
    Living with Losses
    Training in Conflict Resolution
    Summary

11. **YOU CAN FINISH WELL** 143
    A Strong Start in the Calling of God
    Discovering the Stressors of Ministry
    Developing Governing Principles for Finishing Well

APPENDIX

    A. STRESS SYMPTOMS..149

    B. WOLYNIAK SURVEY RESULTS...........................150

    C. WOLYNIAK SURVEY- General Question Results 157

    D. THE PURPOSE of the MENTORING PROGRAM......158

    E. INTERNET RESOURCES......................................162

BIBLIOGRAPHY...165

ACKNOWLEDGEMENTS

I am thankful to have had so many individuals who invested in my life as a young minister and missionary. Their example, love, and trust gave hope and encouragement to continue to follow the Lord in obedience and faith, even in trying times. To them, I am indebted.

The congregation and board of Abundant Life Assembly of God in Monument, Colorado is recognized for their love, counsel, grace, and generosity in allowing me the time to study. A kind thank you is given to Mr. and Mrs. Kenneth Goodrich for the generous use of their cabin, in which much of this book was written.

A special thank you is in order to Dr. Dominic Aquila, who assisted me with his positive attitude, support, and direction during the writing stages on this topic for the dissertation at New Geneva Theological Seminary.

Above all, the writer wishes to thank his wife, Sharon, and their three beautiful daughters, Heather, Heidi, and Christy, for their understanding, assistance, and loving encouragement. They are deeply loved and the joy of my life. You have taught me much, and I am so blessed. Thank you for being a part of the call of God in the pastorate and in serving our Lord on the foreign field.

Author

The journey of Dale Wolyniak has been set with benchmarks of a unique nature. Coming to faith during his college years, Dale pursued his love of the outdoors and was a Park Ranger/Naturalist at Isle Royale National Park, an island in Lake Superior, and at Denali National Park in Alaska. The call to ministry and missions would generate a new direction and path for his future.

Dale earned the Bachelor of Science in Forestry and Wildlife Management from Michigan Technological University, the Master of Arts in Missions from the Assembly of God Theological Seminary, and the Doctor of Ministry from New Geneva Theological Seminary.

Dale has served in the American pastorate for fifteen years. He has been a bi-vocational pastor for two pioneer church plants. Subsequent pastorates included two existing churches in Colorado. The Wolyniak family served as foreign missionaries for ten years. Dale taught at a Bible College in the Marshall Islands of Micronesia, training and equipping young men and women for ministry. Teaching trips were also taken to the Kiribati Islands. The Wolyniaks served in a closed country in Southeast Asia doing pioneer work. Dale was the founder and director of an English Language Center at a University while posted there. It was in this field that Dale experienced the personal testings, isolation, and trials that created an awareness of the need for soul care, commonly called "member care".

The experiences in ministry on the foreign field and the American pastorate ignited the author's passion for this book. Dale recently spent three years as the Member Care Director for a non-profit organization working in Central Asia. Dale has also served as a pastoral counselor at Focus on the Family for pastors and their families.

Dale has spoken on pastoral issues to ministers and those in training in Nepal, the Philippines, Thailand, and in Central Asia. Dale has been an Affiliate Faculty at Colorado Christian University for the past seven years.

Dale and his wife, Sharon, live in Monument, Colorado. They are blessed to have three grown daughters and two grandchildren. Dale still keeps a fly rod handy, and can often be found in some isolated spot exploring the great outdoors.

CHAPTER 1
INTRODUCTION

The Bible says in I Thessalonians 5: 24 "The One who calls you is faithful and He will do it" (New International Version). The New American Standard Bible reads "Faithful is He who calls you, and He also will bring it to pass". What God has started, He will finish. It is the desire of the Father of our Lord Jesus Christ to complete the work He started in our lives. As ministers of the gospel, we recognize that to start out on the journey of faith is just the beginning. To finish well, to complete the task with the goal in mind of bringing to fruition all that God intended, is the objective of our lives.

To finish well, one needs to start with the goal in mind. We are in a race, running to win the prize. Paul the Apostle in Acts 20:24 states "if only I may finish the race and complete the task the Lord Jesus has given me, the task of testifying to the gospel of God's grace". The prize is Christ Himself and the race requires us to pay attention to several important foundational principles. Anyone in this race must be dedicated to strict training of the body and soul. We run not aimlessly, but with a determined goal in mind. Not as one beating the air, but specifically dealing with the issues in front of us. (I Cor. 9:26-27) The goal of lives given to service and ministry of the Word of God, be it the pastorate, the mission field, or another place of service, all require that we stay focused on the goal, stay healthy on the journey, and rely on the provisions that God has made for each of us.

Theological Basis for the Call of God

The first objective is to establish a theological perspective on the general call of God and on the specific call to full time ministry. This will review key word studies and definitions of the call to ministry. In the Old Testament accounts, God calls out individuals like Abraham, Moses, David and the prophets to various tasks of

Finishing Well

leadership. These character studies will be examined with a desire to discover those theological principles that still apply to us today. Our definition of a specific ministry call comes from the historical documents that we have in the New Testament. A precedence for the calling out - the separation for God's holy purposes - is found in the stories of Peter and the apostles as well as Paul and Timothy. Their lives and experiences can shed light for us today on how God calls and directs individuals to fulfill His plans and purposes.

The general call of God is an invitation to all people to come to him in faith, being born again by the Spirit of God. With this general call to salvation comes a corresponding call to do ministry. Everyone whom God has saved should have a ministry. This may mean one of helps, teaching, encouragement, or outreach. Everyone is to be an active participant in the building up of the Kingdom of God. Ephesians 2:8-10 states,

> For by grace have you been saved through faith; and that not
> of yourselves, it is the gift of God; not as a result of works,
> that no one should boast. For we are His workmanship,
> created in Christ Jesus for good works, which God prepared
> beforehand, that we should walk in them.

We have all been saved by grace and now have the joy and opportunity to share our faith and our gifts to minister as servants of the Lord. The special call of God to individuals for positions and offices of ministry is of importance to our study. This is the arena of discerning how God calls, selects, and separates individuals for specific tasks within His church and kingdom. We will examine such topics as how God calls a person to ministry. What does that 'call' look and sound like? How does one heed the call and fulfill its requirements? What are some typical responses to the call of God? What requirements does God have for people He will use in ministry? Does the church body and ecclesiastical organizations have biblical requirements that come to bear on the individual and their personal call?

1 – Introduction

Discovering the Top Causes of Ministerial Stress

It is the emphasis of this paper to discover not only the biblical charge for ministry but also the principles for doing well throughout the years of ministry. We will research the top stressors of ministers today as reported from a variety of ministries such as Focus on the Family, Christianity Today, the Alban Institute, and a survey of current Assemblies of God ministers in the Rocky Mountain District. The surveys come to the conclusion that ministerial stress today is at an all time high and that congregations and governing boards could function in more supportive roles for their ministers.

All ministers face uncharted territory in the years following the initial call of God. There is great joy in being a part of the Lord's family and called as a leader whose life is given to service and love of others in the work of the gospel. With the joy of obedient service also comes demands and expectations by both parishioners and ministers themselves causing added stress and often negative effects on the ministers and their families. Dr Jack Arnold, instructor at New Geneva Theological Seminary, once said in a class in 1998 that pastoral ministry is the "most exciting and rewarding profession in the world, and that it is also the most difficult and unappreciated profession in the world". This calling to ministry has the unique potential to bless the one called as well as bring specific trials and tests of character few others are called to endure.

Background of the Problem

Historically, the church has been given the commission to disciple all nations which requires that leaders are raised up by the Holy Spirit and trained for the task of developing disciples of Jesus Christ. Ministry leadership has many demands placed upon its time and talents within the context of the living Church. Throughout the history of the church, beginning with the record of the Book of Acts, as well as the Epistles, there has been a spiritual tension that has all the potential to hinder if not destroy ministers. Consumed with the passion to share the message of salvation and the need to maintain a balanced life with family and community, the early disciples, especially the apostles, faced a daunting task. In the midst of great

Finishing Well

opportunity to preach the gospel and strengthen the brethren, the leaders and followers of the early church were persecuted, abused, maligned, and threatened by the existing spiritual authorities as well as the political powers of that time. What gave the early church leadership the upper edge to continue to minister and maintain a balanced life ? What is it we should try to discover and perhaps recover from the teachings found in the New Testament that will enable today's ministers to do more than perform - to practice healthy disciplines that will produce fruit pleasing to God ?

In recent times, there has been a steady trend of credentialed ministers and those in active pastoral care to leave the ministry. Today, a new set of stressors are causing some ministers heartache - enough to move them into other fields of service and work. A study made in 1992 by "Leadership Magazine" and published by Christianity Today, Fall edition, surveyed 800 pastors. The report was entitled "What Pastor's Wives Wish Their Churches Knew" (Zoba, 1994). Their findings indicate that there is a growing trend of ministers and spouses who are struggling with both family and marriage relationships as well as ministry expectations. When 94% of pastors feel pressure to have an "ideal family" and with 77% of pastoral spouses feeling the strain "to be an ideal role model for a Christian family", the church leadership team has sufficient stress to create not only domestic problems but to also affect the ministry role in the local congregation. When we are more concerned about maintaining our image than our obedience to the Lord, it is time for reevaluation, redirection, and renewal.

Developing Governing Principles to Assist Ministers

If indeed ministers are suffering undue stress or not adequately handling the demands of this vocation, then it is our task to define and clarify ways to assist them in staying strong in the midst of ministry life.

It is this author's conviction that if we are called to lead then we must be equipped to do so. What does it mean to "finish well" in ministry? Are there some basic governing principles that will help facilitate healthier lifestyles for our ministers?

1 – Introduction

Paul the apostle wrote in his last letter in Second Timothy 4:7, "I have fought the good fight; I have finished the race; I have kept the faith". Paul tells us by his own hand that in the midst of extreme difficulties and setbacks, he was able, by the grace and mercy of God, to finish well the course of ministry God had given him. Again, Paul writes in Acts 20:28, "Keep watch over yourselves and all the flock of which the Holy Spirit has made you overseers". What was it about the Apostle Paul - his circumstances, his friends, his call - that enabled him to finish well? Watching over ourselves as well as the flock will help ensure we obtain a good report of our ministry life.

It is of concern by many denominational boards and churches that many of our ministers are not doing well and are thus leaving their ministry posts and calling. One statement made over the years is that over 50% of ministers are no longer in ministry roles. Many ministerial candidates start out in ministry with great zeal, energy and vision, only to discover that there is more to ministry than perhaps the preparation and preaching of the Gospel. Personal attitudes and preparation of the heart are complex issues that need to be addressed early in ministry preparation at our Bible schools and theological institutes and seminaries. It is wonderful to see people start out following the Lord in ministry, yet there is a need to "finish well". Too many are approaching full-time ministry as a profession, rather than a special, unique calling and equipping of the Lord Jesus Christ. God is not looking for professionals but for people with a genuine, personal relationship with the Lord Jesus Christ. There can be a vast difference between 'working for Jesus, and living for Him.' When there is a clear and well-defined scriptural view of how we are to live for Christ in our culture, then we can most effectively work for Jesus in the equipping and training of disciples.

It is the intent of this author's investigation and research to discover ways to prevent burnout and discouragement that lead to diminished energy and zeal or the eventual leaving the ministry completely. There are numerous books and articles about church growth but few that focus on the growth of the minister. It is proposed that prevention of the harmful effects on ministry life and work can be identified early. Establishing guidelines, developing a network of mentors and friends in accountable relationships, and using various testing materials and assessments will contribute to

Finishing Well

ministerial well-being. Leadership oversight of our ministers can ensure that those who are called to pastoral care ministries "finish well" themselves. Much effort is spent on professional counseling after problems have developed. Maintenance of our ministers in the midst of stress will facilitate better communication and longevity in the ministry.

Summary

Ministry takes place when we have lived what we believe and share that common faith with the people around us. Spiritual ministry is more than proclamation in the pulpit or teaching in the classroom; it is investing in people with our lives. A healthy minister who has been healed, cleansed, and empowered by the Holy Spirit will be the one who not only starts the race, but finishes well. When a person understands the unique call of God to ministry and is aware of the challenges of the journey of faith, then equipped with both the knowledge of one's self and the principles of the inward life, they can achieve success in ministry and life. When a person is diligent in the issues of integrity, faithfulness, a disciplined private life, and accountability, they can remain strong in their calling.

When denominations and church boards acknowledge the special calling and equipping of pastors, missionaries, and ministers, then they too can be used by God to strengthen and enhance the minister in the tasks that accompany this vocation. Stress is a part of any life. We do not intend to eliminate stress but to manage it so as to maintain a balanced life. Ministerial life is more than a profession in which education, theological preparation, and charisma with people are needed. Support systems are needed to assist individuals whom God has called to feed and care for his flock.

God has provided all we need for life and ministry. Let us take what He has provided, put our hand to the plow, and not look back. Let us go from calling to completion, knowing that there is a reward and blessing from the one who calls, Jesus Christ.

CHAPTER 2

GENERAL CALL

Defining the Theological Basis for the General Call of God

Throughout the Bible we find God setting individuals apart for His purposes. It is a significant fact that God goes looking for individuals who are in the midst of life and its activities and chooses them for a special role in His plans. God's intervention in the life of a person is a dynamic statement of His love and acceptance of each individual. This calling to Christ and to His work is about the grace of God and His empowerment - not about ourselves. As we develop spiritually, we bring with us the specific character qualities and inherent gifts and abilities which God now claims for His kingdom. There is a general call to all people to salvation and a right relationship with Almighty God, and then what we will describe in the following chapter as a special call to leadership and ministry.

The General Call

The general call to those whom God would save is the standard call for lost people to respond to the invitation of God; this invitation is based upon the goodness and grace of God alone. The original goal that God had for Israel was that they would be His people - representatives of His grace to the nations of the world (Gen 12.:1-4). This general call, now within the new covenant, is to salvation in Christ, and is separate from the special call to a ministerial position of leadership which would follow such a salvation experience. There is no room for the pride of man, for we are all sinners in need of the Savior's love and redemption.

God is the responsible One who not only initiates the gospel call to man, but Who also has the power and authority to fulfill the demands of that call upon those who have faith to believe. Because we are flawed human beings, our sufficiency must be of God and not of ourselves (2 Cor. 3:5). We are called by God to salvation, and to service in His kingdom, as a result of His gracious love.

The New Bible Dictionary (1962) states that election is "the act of choice whereby God picks an individual or group out of a larger company for a purpose or destiny of His own appointment. The main Old Testament word for this is the verb *'bahar'*, which expresses the idea of deliberately selecting someone or something after carefully considering the alternatives" (p.314). God is actively choosing those people whom He would have in a right relationship with him. This call is general in nature to the populace as a whole. The selectivity of God is based upon His foreknowledge and will. Election is God's gracious choice and sovereign choice, prompted by His own good pleasure (Eph. 1:5, 9), and it is eternal . This calling to salvation is in Christ and no other (Eph. 1:4).

> In the Theological Dictionary of the New Testament, by Kittel (1985), the authors discuss the word translated "call" or "choose". The common Greek meaning of the word *eklegomai*, (in the middle *eklego)* means 'to make a choice,' with various objects, e.g., slaves, payments, or abstract things. The perfect passive means 'choice' or 'chosen.' The verb is mostly used in the LXX (108 times) for the Hebrew root *bhr*. The verb *bhr* ("to choose," "to elect")occurs 164 times in the OT. It expresses a resolve of the divine will with an element of insistence (cf. 1 Sam.12:22). Related terms bring out the implied element of taking, separating, appointing, and knowing. Like the word "to choose," *bhr* denotes choice among possibilities. When objects are chosen, purpose is implied. The same applies in the choice of persons (Gen. 6:2; Exod.18:25), which also carries an element of approval
> (p. 515).

God chooses people within the context of a community, as when He chose Abram out of his community into a faith walk. Israel is God's people by the fact that he chose them out from among all others (Judg. 5:11). God's active choice demands that the chosen ones serve the purposes of God. This election or choice of God carries the responsibility of bearing witness to the nations that there is one God

2 – *General Call*

(Isa. 41:1). The calling of a people is a call to serve God for some divine purpose. The Israelites, as a separated people, were to bear witness to and share their understanding with the nations. "God alone initiates this call, and only a minority (remnant) respond (Joel 2:32)" (The New Bible Dictionary 1962, p. 161).

Old Testament Precedents to the Call of God

The Old Testament holds tremendous value as we seek to comprehend the calling out of a people for God's namesake. The Old Testament reveals that God elected or called Israel to be His people through covenant promise, based on His grace alone. Israel as a people were called out by God to be His chosen vessel to the nations. Scripture reveals the progression of the calling of a man, a family, a clan, a nation, and then a call or invitation to the whole world. Within this general call from God to Himself is the calling of individuals to a special place of leadership, honor, and privilege.

In the beginnings of Genesis, we see God selecting Abram, a man who was willing to leave his homeland after hearing the voice of God and follow His direction by faith. This call is one of redemptive purposes, since God would bless the world through Abraham, as Genesis 12:1-4 states : " and in you all the families of the earth shall be blessed". "The word of Jehovah, by which Abram was called, contained a command and a promise" (Keil and Delitzsch, 2001, p. 123, Vol 1). This call to be a leader of people and to bring them into a faith relationship with God is reiterated in Hebrews 11.8: "By faith Abraham, when he was called, obeyed by going out to a place which he was to receive for an inheritance; he went out, not knowing where he was going". God's call to Abraham is one in which He made His will known in developmental stages. The challenge to Abraham was to obey and follow. Paul the apostle describes Abraham as the father of the faithful (Romans 4:11-12). J.I. Packer (1993) says that "Abraham heeded God's call because he believed God's promise; it was his faith in the promise that was credited to him for righteousness" (Gen. 15:6; Rom. 4:18-22) (Enns, 1977, n.p.).

In the life story of Moses, we see God calling a man out from his occupation to Himself and then into a leadership position in Egypt to be the deliverer of the Hebrew people. Not only does God call

Finishing Well

Moses to be the leader, but He also calls the Hebrew people to be set apart for Himself. Here God calls a learned man, one familiar with the ways of Egypt and in the courts of Pharoah, to a position among the Hebrew slaves as their leader. God would mold Moses over the forty year time period in the desert into a tool for the fulfillment of His promise to have a nation - a people after His name's sake. This calling to Moses was unique in that it was a growth process over time as God dealt with the issues of Moses' character and life, with the goal of using him to lead and guide Israel into the promised land. Again, the individual call of God is made within the context of a community of people. Even though Moses' life call was more of a special call to service, it does stand as an example of the general call to all people to places of service.

New Testament Precedents to the Call of God

In New Testament Greek, there are seventeen words that refer to the concept of "call". The words "call" (192 times), "called" (502 times) and "calling" (43 times) are translated from a number of Greek terms. Of all the words that are translated from the Greek into English, there are a few that have the concept of invitation, summons, calling, or to be called. The semantic range is quite wide, but we will focus on those words and instances that pertain to invitation or summons. Kittel describes the Greek word *kaleo* (148 times) - 'to call' as being "used especially in Luke and Acts, less frequently in Mark and John. It may always be rendered 'to call', but often has the special nuance of divine calling or vocation" (p. 394).

Romans 1:1 reads: "Paul called to be an apostle and set apart"; the first verb is *kletos*, variously translated as called or invited. In Second Thessalonians 1:11, "God may count you worthy of this calling", the word is *klesis*, translated as "call, calling, situation or station in life". In Galatians 1:15, Paul states that God "set me apart and called me"; the word here is *kaleo*. In each of these verses, the word called or calling has the meaning of separated and set apart for a specific job or ministry. The invitation is from the Lord Jesus Christ to Paul to function in the role of minister, apostle to be specific. All three of the above verses use words which almost always have the sense of divine calling (New International Dictionary of New

2 – General Call

Testament Theology, NIDNTT, Volume 1, 1975). The verb *proskaleo* is used 29 times in the New Testament and is translated "to call or summon". Acts 13:2 reads, " for the work to which I have called them"; and Acts 2:39, " for all whom the Lord our God will call."

Summary

In the New Testament church there was a general call to repentance that birthed people into the Kingdom of God. In the Gospel accounts, the Lord gives an open invitation to individuals to know Him, as is the case of Nicodemus in John 3. Here is a conversation between a learned religious leader and Christ Jesus on the topic of being born again. It is with interest to us that Jesus must clarify what He is talking about to this spiritual man of standing. Jesus is both personable and patient as He allows the truth of His words and the explanation of this call to salvation to penetrate the mind and heart of Nicodemus. This dialogue is considered a call to accept or reject an invitation to follow Christ, the Anointed One.

Paul would write the Thessalonians about how God chose them to be saved through the work of the Holy Spirit and through belief in the truth (2 Thess.2:13-14). This call brought with it the expectation and energy necessary to do the work of ministry. Ephesians 2:8-10 expresses the work of ministry which is a goal of the Lord for every believer: "For we are God's workmanship, created in Christ Jesus to do good works, which God prepared in advance for us to do." Second Thessalonians 1:11 continues this thought: "With this in mind, we constantly pray for you, that our God may count you worthy of his calling, and that by his power he may fulfill every good purpose of yours and every act prompted by your faith." Again, we see that God is choosing, calling, and electing to Himself those who would be His people for His purposes. God intends for His people, called by His name, to be about the Father's business, even supplying the power in which to minister.

The ministry of the Christian is designed by God to focus on the proclamation and presentation of the gospel of grace to all mankind. Along with the proclaiming of the free gift of salvation in Christ, there was to be an involvement with the lives of people from a Christian perspective. All believers are to invest their lives and work

Finishing Well

in blessing others, and in doing so, minister to their community what God has placed in their hearts. As the church, composed of individuals with a salvation experience, moves to impact the community, its membership is to become salt and light by its deeds of kindness for those it encounters. It is by the means of grace that the people of the new covenant minister to the common physical, emotional, and spiritual needs of its families. Rick Warren, in his book *The Purpose Driven Life,* comments: "God has a unique role for you to play in His family. This is called your 'ministry', and God has gifted you for this assignment. "A spiritual gift is given to each of us as a means of helping the entire church." (1 Cor. 12:7 NLT, p. 134).

Scripture indicates that God gave gifts unto men, and that He distributed these gifts as He willed to His church (1 Cor. 12:14). This gifting, be they specific spiritual gifts as First Corinthians 12 & 14 indicates, or the general talents, abilities, and personal giftings each person inherits or develops, are to be used for the glory of God. If God has indeed given gifts to men, then His goal must be that they are used in ministry to those in the community and the church. God wants something in return for the investment He has placed in each person. As in the story of the talents given to the stewards (Matt. 25:14-30), there does come a day of accounting, when each man's use of his gifts are reviewed and rewarded. The Lord wants each person to participate in ministry.

In John Walvoord's (1985) commentary on First Corinthians 7:20-24, (Enns, 1977, n.p.) he states that when it comes to obedience to Christ :

> A Christian's vocational situation is a matter of little consequence (if status can be changed, well and good; if not, it is not a matter for worry). What matters is that every Christian should realize he is Christ's slave and needs to render obedience to Him. Every vocation then becomes Christian service performed for the Master (cf. Eph. 6:5-8). The fact that God had called each one to a vocation and sought from each one faithful service in that calling elevated and sanctified both

2 – *General Call*

the work and the worker. A Christian could then 'live in peace' (v. 15) in his calling and carry it out as one responsible to God.

It appears that one's vocational situation, job, or occupation has little to do with being effective for the Lord. One is to perform and minister in obedient faith no matter what one's station in life may be.

In the book of First Peter 4:10, it is recorded that "each one should use whatever gifts he has received to serve others". As we minister in the area of our gifting, others are served and the Lord is glorified. This approach allows individuals to focus on their gifts - be it teaching, preaching, administration, or any of a number of gifts, and contribute their part to the whole of ministry life within the community of faith. This view may indeed assist the general Christian population in finding their calling to service by evaluating and recognizing their spiritual and natural giftings.

As was common in the Old Testament dispensation, the Word of God calls for full participation by all. The change in the New Testament is that all the people are " a chosen people, a royal priesthood, a holy nation, a people belonging to God, that you may declare the praises of him who called you out of darkness into his wonderful light"(1 Pet. 2:9-10). By examining the general call of salvation, we see that God invites people to a relationship with Himself, offering them salvation and fellowship through Jesus Christ. No longer is the call to do ministry given to a select few priests and Levites, but all may have the general call to honor God. It appears that all are called to have a ministry - to function as ambassadors for Christ wherever they may be located - and to honor God with whatever gifts and in whatever opportunity may present itself to bless all people and further His kingdom.

CHAPTER 3

SPECIAL CALL TO MINISTRY

Within the economy of God, there are those men and women who are selected by the Lord to be servant leaders for the community of the faithful. The dynamic person of Paul the apostle recognized the will of God in the call when he wrote: "Paul, an apostle of Jesus Christ, by the will of God, and Timothy our brother" (Col.1:1). This calling to leadership is distinct and separate from the general call to all Christians to have an active participation in ministry. The calling of God to the ministry is the highest calling one could receive, as the minister handles the Word of Life and administers grace and hope to the hurting. Henry Brandt, co-author of *The Power of the Call* (1997) said :

> You are the custodian of the most important information in the world....You are a specialist in what God has to say to people through the Bible. Your divine calling far supersedes all other professions. Your presence and impact has eternal consequences in the world (p.22).

When we begin to realize the impact the Word of God has on people's lives, we are in a better position to assess the special calling of God's spokesman.

Understanding the call to ministerial life will assist those who enter into full time ministry, helping them to realize that it is the Lord of the work who has called them to do the work of the Lord. This understanding can help clarify many of the issues that arise concerning this unique position given by God. Howard F. Sugden and Warren W. Wiersbe in their book, *When Pastors Wonder How* (1973), state:

> The work of the ministry is too demanding and difficult for a man to enter it without a sense of divine calling. Men enter and leave the ministry usually because they lack a sense of divine urgency. Nothing less than a definite call from God could ever give a man success in the ministry (p. 105).

Finishing Well

The ministry is not just another profession where natural talents find a place of service. It is a divine calling of God upon the heart and life of a Christian whom God has set apart for His purposes and glory. In evaluating the call to special service as a leader in the church, we look first to the Word of God for its statements about this matter. The call to full time ministry is the reference point from which we must measure all activities and results.

Old Testament Call to Leadership

Early on the in the Old Testament, we have record of God calling individuals to leadership positions within the community of faith. The unique setting apart of men like Abraham, Moses, Elijah and David are just a few of those whom God selected and invited to follow Him. Each of these individuals was chosen by God for a unique position in the spiritual and political formation of the nation of Israel.

The Calling of Abraham

When we look at the scriptures that speak of a selection process, we find that God calls out individuals from their communities to serve Him in a more specific role in leadership. When Abraham (Gen.12:1-6) is called out by God, it is for the eventual establishment of a people who will be a witness in the world of the One true and living God. The promises of God are given to Abraham, who in the midst of his people's idolatry, is given a unique opportunity to obey and trust Almighty God. Abraham builds an altar (Gen.12:8) and then leaves his home and community to follow the voice and direction of God. The selection was of God, not of Abraham. He who would become the father of a nation shows two character traits of biblical greatness. "The journey's destination was a mystery to Abraham . . . leaving . . . and demands both total obedience and trust" (MacDonald, 2000, p. 70). Abraham displayed obedience in that he went where God instructed him, and he showed trust in believing that provision would be made for his every need. The possession of obedience and trust is, according to MacDonald, a mid-course correction in the life of Abraham where God speaks,

3 – Special Call to Ministry

intervenes, and changes the course and direction of a man whom He would use in a much broader plan.

Abraham was not a perfect man when God began to work in his life, but he was willing and obedient to the Lord. It was this obedience from the heart that God saw and rewarded by fulfilling His divine promises. This man's journey of faith as recorded in Genesis provides us with a testimony of the development of a relationship between a called man and the Lord. Abraham would become a father of many nations in spite of the fact that in the flesh he tried to fulfill the promise of God for a son. In the life story of Abraham, we have lessons in leadership of both a positive and negative nature. We can learn from both if we are willing to listen. The purpose of the call to Abraham would be fulfilled amidst many trials and setbacks with his two sons, Isaac and Ishmael. God went looking for an individual whom He could use for His glory, and He found that person in Abraham.

The calling of Abraham from Ur of the Chaldees and bringing him into the promised land of Canaan was fulfilled when God called Israel out of Egypt under Moses. The New Bible Dictionary (1962) states that God was :

> renewing the Abrahamic covenant with them in an amplified form at Sinai and setting them in the promised land as their national home (Exod. 3:6-10; Deut. 6:21-23; Ps. 105). Each of these acts of choice is also described as God's call, *i.e.* a sovereign utterance of words and disposal of events by which God summoned, in the one case, Abraham, and in the other, Abraham's seed, to acknowledge him as their God and live to him as his people (Isa. 51:2; Hos. 11:1;). Israelite faith looked back to these two acts as having created the nation (*cf.* Isa. 43:1; Acts 13:17) (p. 315).

The call of God to Abraham was to fulfill the larger purposes of God in building a nation who would follow and obey the one true and living Jehovah God. It was the sovereign choice of God and not the will of man that led to the development of the nation of Israel.

Finishing Well

The Calling of Moses

The Old Testament book of Exodus (Exod. 3-12) records the calling of the man Moses from the midst of Egyptian servitude, having been placed by the providence of God in Pharoah's own household. Moses' past experience as a commander under Pharoah did not prepare him for the encounter with God years later in the desert. At the burning bush, Moses is confronted with claims of God upon his life. In a series of questions and refusals that reveal Moses' reluctance, God answers with reassurances: He will be with Moses (3:11); His name is " I am that I am" (3:13); He will provide a staff to help Israel believe (4:1); and He will give Aaron as a spokesperson for Moses (4:10). In the end Moses' reply is "Oh Lord, please send someone else to do it" (4:13). The reluctance of Moses to the call of God upon his life is repeated as the story unfolds. For the time being, Moses is obedient and begins the process of following God's direction for Israel's salvation and deliverance from the bondage of Egypt. In the future, Moses will often complain to the Lord about the people he was called to lead (Exod. 5:22), and it will be these same people who will receive the instructions from Moses the lawgiver.

When we look at the life of Moses and the special call to service for the Lord, we see that God chooses a man who has already developed leadership ability in the courts of Pharoah. God then has to take Moses out of Egypt for forty years in the desert to prepare him to lead His chosen people. The final forty years of the life of Moses as lawgiver and deliverer show us that the call of God upon the life of Moses is constantly being tested, and that the commitment of this man is proven time and again. God is faithful to Moses and He again reveals that it is the hand of Almighty God that delivered the Israelites and kept them the forty years in the wilderness. God supplied all the needs of His called people and its leadership. God even supplied Moses with the seventy elders (Num:11:16). Clowney (1995, p.206) states that even these elders were "set apart to their office by a gift of the Spirit. They were not only judges but also spokesmen for the people (Deut. 14:12; 21:19; Exod. 3:16; 4:29; 24:1-2)".

Old Testament history shows us that God calls people for special offices and functions within the economy of the spiritual formation and management of His people. We have the calling of

3 – *Special Call to Ministry*

prophets, priests, and kings. These men and women were called out by God for special assignments to accomplish the plan of God - that of nation building. God, as the Great Shepherd (Ps. 80:1), would work through these select individuals as they spoke, wrote, directed, and led the Hebrew people. This under-shepherd role would accomplish great things for the people of God (Num.11:24-30; Jer.23:1-4; Ezek. 34).
God chose these individuals to specific tasks for the strengthening of His own people and for the wider purposes of blessing the world with His redemptive love.

The Calling of the Prophets

Like Moses, Elijah (1 Kings 17) is a man whom God called to oppose Baal worship that had stolen the heart of Israel. Elijah is sustained by God's provision through the raven and the widow (1 Kings 17:6,9) to show that God is all-powerful. In the midst of ministry, the widow's son is restored to life, resulting in the expression, "Now I know that you are a man of God" (17:24). Further definitive acts of power by God through His servant-prophet Elijah result in the return of Israel to Jehovah, and are demonstrated in the confrontation of the prophets of Baal at Mount Carmel (1 Kings 18:16).

Other prophets like Isaiah (6:1-6) and Jeremiah (1:5) are called by God to warn of impending judgment upon the nation due to disobedience. Along with the warning, they also bring a message of restoration and hope. In discussions on Isaiah 6:8, Keil (2001) says, "The prophet is here relating his first call to the prophetic office and not his call to one particular duty" (p. 132, vol. 7). It is to be noticed that Isaiah responds to the Lord's question with an eagerness of commitment and willingness to go. For Isaiah, the call to office as messenger to Israel would be in vain, as the people's hearts were hardened, ears dulled, and eyes dimmed to the realities of God's goodness and grace. The hardening had been in process for some time, and now God is sending forth His messenger with dire consequences for the people. This divine calling of God is described by Isaiah in vivid detail, giving us a view of the holiness and glory of God. Isaiah responded to the voice of God and volunteered. The Lord clarified the dimensions of that divine call to ministry with the result

Finishing Well

in full view, prior to Isaiah's going out to speak for God. The only question Isaiah has at this extraordinary moment was, "How long, oh Lord?"

The Calling to King Saul and King David

The special call of God to Saul - and then David - as king of Israel, reveals the sovereignty of God's choice. After the period of the Judges, Israel begins requesting a king so they can be like other nations (1 Sam. 8:4-22). God speaks through His prophet Samuel to anoint Saul as king (1 Sam. 9:15-11:14). It is interesting to realize that God wants to be king of His people, but relents and gives them their request to be like the other nations, along with the trouble that will come with such a leader. As time elapses, Saul proves to be an ineffective king, and God raises up David instead (1 Sam. 1 15). God will take the role of king away from Saul: "But now your kingdom will not endure; the Lord has sought out a man after his own heart and appointed him leader of his people, because you have not kept the Lord's command" (13:14).

The calling of David from being a shepherd of sheep to a shepherd over Israel is all of God's choosing. He chooses the household of Jesse (1 Sam. 16) to supply the next king. "I have chosen one of his sons to be king" (16:1). The selection process narrows the choice down: " The Lord does not look at the things man looks at. Man looks at the outward appearance, but the Lord looks at the heart" (16:7). Eventually, after seven sons pass by Samuel, David, the eighth, is selected: "then the Lord said, 'Rise and anoint him; he is the one"(16:12). The Lord calls, or selects David, the youngest son of Jesse, to be king over all Israel. The ascension to the throne will be a difficult and traumatic one for David, as Saul is still in power and antagonistic towards David. It is said of King David that "he was a man after God's own heart." This statement, made in view of David's many sins and mistakes, shows us that God's choice was no mistake, and that God can work in the midst of one's learning curve. Psalms 78:70-72 explains the transformation of David due to the call of God:

He chose David his servant and took him from the sheep pens; from tending the sheep he brought him to be the shepherd of

3 – Special Call to Ministry

his people Jacob, of Israel his inheritance. And David shepherded them with integrity of heart; with skillful hands he led them.

The calling out of individuals in the Old Testament is done in the context of community life and for the various purposes that God designs. The prophets spoke the oracles of God to their culture to bring them back to the One and Only God (Isa. 41); the priests were called and appointed by God to offer up sacrifices in the tabernacle and temple of Jehovah God; the kings were called out to lead and give direction to the people of covenant promise. In all these instances, it is God who selects individuals and works in and through them to achieve His plans and purposes. Those obedient to the call find the blessings of God, as well as difficulties and trials that challenge their commitment to the calling of God. Faithfulness is rewarded by the Lord to those who stay by their post and fulfill their calling in a spirit of humility and grace.

New Testament Call to Leadership

When Jesus uses the word 'to follow', the Greek *akoloutheo*, it is the response of those called that is described as following (e.g. Luke 5:11). When Jesus called the early disciples, "He called man with a divine authority as God himself called the prophets of the Old Testament (Matt.1:16; 8:22)" (Brown, 1975, p. 482). The gospels record the calling of the first disciples who would, in due course, become the apostles of the early church.

The Calling of the Twelve

The twelve disciples are called by Christ to follow Him, (Matt. 4:18-22; Mark. 1:16-20; Luke.5:1-11; John 1:40-42) which involves a giving up of the old obedience to the law and a coming into a new obedience of faith. This call to discipleship involves being set apart to salvation and fellowship, which brings with it the possibility of suffering with Christ as well. The call to discipleship to Jesus "always included the call to service" (Brown, 1975, p. 489). According to Mark 1:17 and Luke 5:10, the disciples are to be fishers of men. As

Finishing Well

the Gospels unfold the development of this band of men into true disciples, Jesus Christ also reveals more of His own true nature and power. The same power and authority for a healing and deliverance ministry that is possessed by Jesus Christ is now transferred to the apostles (Luke 9:1-9) as a sign of the coming of the kingdom of God.

In the beginning of Jesus' ministry, John the apostle records in his gospel (John 1:29-51) the invitation to follow the Lord. In Alexander Bruce's book, *The Training of the Twelve* (1995), he states:

> What an insignificant event in the history of the church, not to say of the world, this first meeting of Jesus of Nazareth with five humble men, Andrew, Peter, Philip, Nathanael, and another unnamed! It actually seems almost too trivial to find a place even in the evangelic narrative. For we have here to do not with any formal solemn call to the great office of the apostleship, or even with the commencement of an uninterrupted discipleship, but at the utmost with the beginnings of an acquaintance with and of faith in Jesus on the part of certain individuals who subsequently became constant attendants on His person, and ultimately apostles of His religion (p. 1).

Although this 'call' is quiet and not done with any great fanfare or ceremony, we do find the total grace of God, His divine sovereignty working to accomplish His plans with human instruments of His choosing. The outworking of that initial call to follow will show that from:
> the time of their being chosen, indeed, the twelve entered on a regular apprenticeship for the great office of apostleship, in the course of which they were to learn, in the privacy of an intimate daily fellowship with their Master, what they should be, do, believe, and teach, as His witnesses and ambassadors to the world" (Bruce,1995, p. 30).

With the selection of these twelve, Jesus is preparing them for the mission of the Father. The Gospels reveal the often slow development

3 – Special Call to Ministry

of the apostle's thinking and the practical outworking of the gospel of Christ's love to the lost of their day.

It is the apostles who are to be the agents used by the Lord to declare His gospel to the world. These messengers are called and equipped by Jesus Himself. They receive the authority and anointing of the Holy Spirit to transmit, through word and deed, the glorious message of salvation in Christ alone. The special call to which the apostles obey brings forth the results of a growing body of believers redeemed in the name of the Lord. These change agents were turning the world upside down as they proclaimed the message they had taken to heart.

In the Great Commission of Christ in Matthew 28:19-20, we have the command of Christ to the apostles to "Go into all the world, and make disciples, teaching them to obey all things He has commanded them." We are speaking here of the unique and divine call of God for 'full-time ministry'. This is the leadership role of those described in Ephesians 4:11-13 who are called to "prepare God's people for works of service, so that the body of Christ may be built up until we all reach unity in the faith and in the knowledge of the Son of God and become mature, attaining to the whole measure of the fullness of Christ." It is these agents of change, leaders called by God, whom we want to understand. God calls men and women to witness His sacrificial love and to preach the gospel of Jesus Christ. God uses people, weak instruments though they may be, to proclaim the message of eternal life. Ministry leaders of God's church are those whom He has selected and called into a place of servant leadership.

It is God's plan for redeemed men to share their faith with others for their eternal benefit. The goal of God is to reach the lost and disciple the found through the ever-expanding outreach and ministry of His people and the organization of His church. The heart of God is that "anyone who trusts in him will never be put to shame" (Rom. 10:11), and that "everyone who calls on the name of the Lord will be saved" (Rom. 10:13).

The record of the New Testament states that saved men are to be instruments of God's righteousness and grace. God chooses to work through his people to perform His salvation work in restoring fallen mankind to a right relationship. Thus is born the purpose for

Finishing Well

ministry: reaching and keeping people in the will and work of the Spirit of God, for His glory and their redemption.

The Calling of Paul the Apostle

Paul the apostle is recorded as having been saved and called simultaneously (Acts 9:11-31). His ministry to the Gentiles enlisted all his experiences and knowledge as a trained Hebrew scholar and leader. He received instruction from the Lord and spent years preparing himself for an ongoing ministry. We see here that the acceptance of the call to minister does change the course of one's life. Paul goes on to experience the blessing of God in establishing churches and converts in the Christian faith. The way of Jesus for the minister, Paul, is one of suffering and trials, but God is shown to be "faithful to those whom he calls" (1 Thess. 5:24).

Paul sees himself as a servant, a love slave, an apostle by the will of God and not man. Paul uses the Greek word *doulos* (Phil.1:1; Titus 1:1), translated 'slave', when he speaks of his relation to Christ. In this role, he is obedient and willing to die for the gospel cause. To take up the call of ministry means for Paul a total change in perspective and love. Zealous for the law and Judaism above all his equals, Paul is humbled into the dust and finally recognizes that he has been persecuting Christ Himself, and not just the followers of the Christian way. Revelation makes a way into the heart of Paul, bringing about regeneration and eventually a ministry of reconciliation. Apostle Paul says in Colossians 1:25, "I have become its servant (the church) by the commission God gave me to present to you the word of God in its fullness."

God had a plan for Paul and that plan would involve the issue of faith and trust on the part of Paul. Any ministry call brings with it the definitive moment of understanding that God Himself is drawing a person into a walk of faith in the midst of fire, misunderstanding, and even rejection. "Going not knowing" has been the call through the ages, from Abraham and Paul to today's gospel preachers and ministers.

For most individuals, the initial call of God to ministry is often more of a process of discovery and growth than a "Damascus road experience". This is not to say that God does not call specifically in

3 – Special Call to Ministry

time and space to an individual. He surely does, and is capable of calling under any circumstances; generally in the experience of the church, though, God develops a person into a useful vessel by smaller increments and experiences. The testing process so common to us all brings greater challenges to develop our faith and character. The special calling of God to be a minister is an internal work of the Lord that has outward expressions and acknowledgments. There usually comes a time when the desire of a person's heart is so inclined to follow the Lord in obedience that the passion and purpose of life is to surrender all for the opportunity for ministry. To share the plan of salvation, to preach the message of the Savior's love, to proclaim the invitation to all becomes an all-consuming choice of the heart.

The Calling of Paul and Timothy

While Paul becomes an apostle for the work of the Lord, we find him with a team of others, including a young man named Timothy (Acts 16:1), who will eventually become a minister himself. The Paul-Timothy model is an excellent example of the training process of one chosen by God. This is an on-the-job training program so that wherever Paul the apostle goes, be it Corinth or Ephesus, Timothy is there as well (Acts 18:5; 19:22). Instruction and the practical outworking of ministry life and outreach are a daily diet for young Timothy. Scripture indicates that Timothy (1 Tim. 4:1-16) became a fine leader in the church, one who could be trusted, who was respected and accepted as a minister in his own right. The choosing of Timothy was the Lord's working through His apostle and in the context of ministry life.

Requirements of Leadership from the Epistles

The New Testament gives the standard requirements for ministers today. The closest biblical call to the pastorate is that which we find in the life and ministry of young Timothy. Here we have a 'man of God' who undergoes not a burning bush of a Moses, or the voice of God on a Damascus road like Apostle Paul, but the gentle development and illumination of the calling of God. It is in the Pastoral Epistles that Paul gives specific instructions on the qualifications for elders, bishops, and deacons (1Tim. 3:1-7; Tit. 1:5-9). By reviewing these passages to the early church, we are able to develop an understanding of the general requirements for a person who is called to the ministry. Foundational to the call of God is the salvation experience, a personal life of holiness, and the gifting of the Holy Spirit upon the individual. It appears that in the New Testament Church, elders were singled out based upon their experience, maturity in the faith, and ability to teach the Word of God. The early church functioned with a variety of styles of organizational guidance and leadership. These servant leaders were not only to lead and give direction to the body of Christ, but were to be examples of the grace of God in Christ. These early church bodies were generally governed by a plurality of elders, and yet in Titus we see that the church functioned without the elders, with only Titus being their pastor. A shared responsibility for the ministry of the Word of God and the care of the people was the norm when Timothy and Titus were written.

J.I. Packer (Enns,1996, n.p.) expresses the honor that comes with the high calling of God to the minister when he writes :

> If any one would be deemed a true minister of the Church, he must *first* be duly called; and, *secondly*, he must answer to his calling; that is, undertake and execute the office assigned to him. This may often be observed in Paul, who, when he would approve his apostleship, almost always alleges a call, together with his fidelity in discharging the office. If so great a minister of Christ dares not arrogate to himself authority to be heard in the Church, unless as having been appointed to it by the command of his Lord, and faithfully performing what has been entrusted to him, how great the effrontery for any man, devoid of one or both of them, to demand for himself such honor.

This honorable calling of pastor, or minister, is one in which God is working to accomplish through men the plans of heaven itself. God is the one initiating the invitation for man to join Him in the gospel ministry. This authority is given from God to man; man does not take it on himself to rule or lead others. In speaking of Jesus as our high priest, and then the special office and calling to be the high

3 – *Special Call to Ministry*

priest, Hebrews 5:4 states that "No one takes this honor upon himself; he must be called by God, just as Aaron was." In the work of God, it is God alone who establishes people in places of authority for the expansion of His kingdom on earth.

Paul Enns, in his book, *The Moody Handbook of Theology* describes the words used in the New Testament for the church's leadership :

> While the church is a living organism, it is also an organization, involving offices and function. There are two designated offices in the New Testament church. The office of *elder* (Gk. presbuteros) emphasizes maturity and dignity and normally denotes an older person. Elders were appointed as leaders in the local churches (1 Tim. 5:17; Tit. 1:5). The term *bishop* or *overseer* (Gk. episkopos) denotes the work of shepherding by the elder (1 Tim. 3:1). The terms are basically synonymous, although elder signifies the office whereas overseer emphasizes function. The work of the elders involved teaching (1 Tim. 5:17), ruling (1 Tim. 5:17), shepherding, nurturing, and caring for the flock (1 Tim. 3:1). Their qualifications are listed in 1 Timothy 3:1–7 (Enns, 1996, p.111).

Organization of the church requires leadership roles for the operation and general well-being of its constituents. Terms used today such as pastor, elder, minister, or other terms, help identify the functional role of leadership in the church. The word deacon is descriptive of those who would serve within the body of Christ at a different level and for a different purpose (Acts 6).

The New Testament clearly identifies those specifically called of God and those whom God equips for special service to the church and to the world. The Ephesians 4:11 passage says, "It is He who gave some to be apostles, some to be prophets, some to be evangelists, and some to be pastors and teachers." Within this calling comes a reassurance that God is the one who has selected, set aside, and equipped for His divine purposes. In this passage, the purpose of selection is to prepare God's people for works of service for the building up of the body of Christ. When individuals acknowledge that

Finishing Well

the Lord Jesus Christ has set His seal upon them for the building up of the body of Christ and for the expansion of the kingdom of the redeemed, then they can labor in love even in the most trying circumstances. It is the call of God that will keep them going strong, even in the midst of suffering, trial, or isolation. It is that inner working of the Spirit in the heart of ministers that sustains them, giving them hope, assurance, and the power to finish well in the work that God has selected for them. Without this definitive work of grace in the heart of a minister, the work becomes laborious, tedious, and often just another job. God has called us to a higher calling. Let us pursue His ways which are far above our ways.

Contemporary Authors

We have a contemporary review of the issues of a divine call by Bob Sewell, founder of SonScape Ministries. He states that 40% of ministers question their call to ministry and at least 30 % often think about leaving the ministry (London, 2003, p. 195). If there is this much questioning going on in ministers' lives as to their vocation as ministers, then perhaps there is a need to explore and appraise what Scripture says on the topic of a divine call to the ministry. If ministry life is to continue in a healthy direction, then we need to have a solid basis for the initial call to ministry.

While we recognize that all are called to participate in some form of ministry, there are specific roles that God has chosen for the welfare and well-being of the body of Christ. Edmund P. Clowney (1995) in his book *The Church*, states that "The governing of the church is a shared responsibility. . . Without the support of the whole body, the work of those with greater gifts for leadership would not be effective, or even possible. We submit to the authority of the whole while exercising our own" (p. 205). The gift and calling of leadership over the church is one of function and not entitlement or rulership; it works best when all participate with the grace and wisdom of God.

John MacArthur, editor of his book, *Rediscovering Pastoral Ministry* (1995), enlists the help of others to write on a variety of topics that concern the ministry of pastors. James M. George discusses the 'Call to Pastoral Ministry', and examines the four major

3 – Special Call to Ministry

assessments to discerning a genuine call to ministry. He states that it is the confirmation by God and others; the abilities of the person; the longings and desires to be a part of ministry; and the life of integrity. Each of these four areas reveal the heart of the call of God (p.106).

In discussing the confirmation of both God and man, there is a need for the local church to affirm and accept current ministry efforts of the individual. Paul the Apostle (Acts 16:2) states that Timothy 'had the laying on of hands of the presbytery' as an indication of their support for his call to service. This recognition by the body of believers is their affirmation of the call of God and is the first of four signs that James M. George (1995, p.102) puts forth. God also affirms a call to ministry by providentially arranging circumstances in which the candidate becomes involved. One's abilities are the second sign in recognizing the call of God and "must be more than natural talent; (they) should include the gift of God to the individual" (George, 1995, p. 108). George describes three general categories of abilities necessary for the ministry: instructional, pastoral, and administrative. The third sign of God's call is a longing or desire to be involved in ministry. First Timothy 3:1 uses the word 'aspire', which means to "stretch oneself out in order to touch or to grasp something; to reach after or desire something" (Swanson, 1997, n.p.). There should be a strong desire to be in ministry; so much so that it is the driving force of one's life. No other vocation or job will satisfy. The last sign is possessing a life of integrity (George, 1995, p. 112), that of personal character and conduct. If one is to be used by God, he or she must possess a life that is holy and pleasing to the Lord. This requires one to continually develop personal inner discipline, which results in a holy life. These four areas agree with the scriptural pattern and general guidelines we have in the New Testament.

Summary

The special call of the Lord to individuals is the sovereign choice of God for a set purpose. This calling is of a spiritual nature and is recognized by both the recipient of the call and those to whom they would minister. There are examples in both the Old and New Testaments of individuals whom God chose for specific purposes of leadership and spiritual guidance. We recognize that God chose men

Finishing Well

like Abraham, Moses, and David to lead Israel, and prophets like Isaiah and Jeremiah to proclaim the message of the Lord to a backslidden Israel. Each instance of calling or being chosen by God is precipitated by a need for someone to fulfill a role in the long-term plan of God. The Lord calls with a purpose in mind, for a developing relationship with Himself as He leads the called person to proclaim, receive, give direction, and obediently follow His instructions.

From Genesis to Revelation, the Bible speaks of a group of men and women who are called specifically to a ministerial position, to serve both people and the Lord. We recognize that God calls and equips people for a variety of tasks and roles within the gospel outreach and the building up of the body of Christ.

In describing the call of the minister, author Joel Nederhood, in *The Preacher and Preaching* (Logan, 1986, p. 33), writes of this unique call: "It is one's conviction that God would have him faithfully proclaim the Word of God." This conviction of the Spirit was on the apostle Paul when he said, "Yet when I preach the gospel, I cannot boast, for I am compelled to preach. Woe is me if I do not preach the gospel!"(1 Cor. 9:16). To the one called to the pastorate, there will always be a strong personal conviction to proclaim the one and only message of the Bible with compassion, humbleness, and courage. Nederhood reminds us that the call of God develops over time as the Lord builds into our lives the wisdom, grace, and power to perform His callings to His Church. Because the call is such an individual and an internal work, there are a great variety of expressions as to what that call is. We can say that when God calls, He gifts that person for the responsibilities that come with the designation of the ministry role.

For a minister of the gospel to finish well, he needs to have a biblical and spiritual understanding of the call. To finish well, one needs to start on a right foundation and run the course with the goal in mind. The call is from the Lord Jesus Christ, and in that calling is His provision for all things we have need of for ministry and life. When we remember the fresh touch of God upon our lives, recalling the steps of faith we took to obey the call, and the corresponding blessing of God, we can gain strength and grace to continue on in our ministry, so as to finish well. There are new demands and opportunities that come to the one called by God and this will require adjustments in

3 – Special Call to Ministry

one's understanding of the call of God. Re-evaluation of how one handles ministry trials and challenges is essential to coping with life in the modern-day pastorate.

Our role in the Kingdom of God is that of recognition of our call to special service and the completion of that calling. Os Guiness, in *The Long Journey Home* (2001) expresses it well when he says: "Indeed, nothing better illuminates the entire journey of life and faith, and in particular the special calling of finishing well, than the issue of purpose" (p. 206). Finding our God-given purpose and then making every effort to fulfill it in the context of biblical faith and action will ensure we finish well.

CHAPTER 4

TOP STRESSORS OF MINISTERS TODAY

When Jesus called his disciples to go into all the world, preach the gospel, and make disciples, he was setting them on a course of action that would tax their mental, physical, and spiritual resources. Unless they would abide in Him (John 15), they would be ineffective and find only failure and frustration. Abiding in Him would result in fruit, joy, and the growth of the Kingdom of God. As it turned out they had a little of both as the early church shared the message of salvation in difficult situations. Today, ministers face similar challenges, tests, and trials, much like those of their earlier New Testament counterparts. It is of concern today that we are seeing unprecedented numbers of ministers leaving their posts from churches around the country. We will concentrate now on pastoral stressors as our primary subject. We will investigate a variety of national and denominational surveys of clergy health and ministry-related topics. Member care to those in ministry has become essential if our ministers are to remain strong in their calling.

In the last chapter, we discussed the important subject of the special call of God to the ministry. If one does not have a genuine call to ministry, then perhaps when the going gets tough or pastoral life becomes routine, the minister leaves for other occupations. It is significant when 40% of ministers claim to struggle with a specific call to ministry. If ministry is viewed as just another occupation and there is no 'holy concept of calling', then indeed we may be able to justify this erosion within the ranks of the pastorate. When ministry becomes just another profession, then the tension and demands can have an adverse effect that would contribute to the decision to leave the ministry role.

With over 375,000 churches in the United States today, we must ask the question within the context of our changing society as to why there appears to be a greater number of ministers changing their vocation. All of life and work has a certain level of stress and tension,

Finishing Well

but perhaps more so with the man or woman in full-time ministry. Several recent denominational surveys as well as some that were from a broader perspective shed light on the difficulties that pastors are facing today.

Stress Defined

When we approach the subject of ministry-related tension or stress, we need to identify what this term implies. "The American Medical Association defines stress as any interference that disturbs a person's mental and physical well-being. However, we commonly define stress as a response to conditions and events, both routine and out of the ordinary" (Inlander and Moran, 1996, p. 1). *Taber's Cyclopedic Medical Dictionary* defines stress:

> In medicine, the result produced when a structure, system, or organism is acted upon by forces that disrupt equilibrium or produce strain. In health care, the term denotes the physical and psychological forces that are experienced by individuals. It is generally believed that biological organisms require a certain amount of stress to maintain their well-being. However, when stress occurs in quantities that the system cannot handle, it produces pathological changes (Thomas, 1989, p. 1763).

Chronic stress in the general population shows up by contributing to 50 percent of all illnesses; 80 percent of all visits to the medical doctors; and seven in ten adults who said that stress was felt in a typical day at work (Inlander and Moran, 1996, p. 1). With such widespread responses to stress, clergy are not immune to the same issues as the general population. Stress affects the emotional, mental, and physical well-being of individuals and shows up in a variety of well-documented symptoms.

To manage stress and live healthy and productive lives, one needs to identify, clarify, and assess those areas of life that create the chronic stress that leads to burnout. Work habits, the work environment, and the interpersonal relationships we have all contribute to our stress levels. To change the way we live and work,

4- Top Stressors of Ministers Today

an appropriate evaluation of our work schedules and their effects on us is in order.

National Survey Results on Pastoral Stress

The minister's magazine, *Leadership Journal,* conducted a survey in 1997 to gather information on pastors' work habits (Church Research Report, CRR, 1997, p. 28). In their random sample of 1,999 subscribers, they had a return of 580 questionnaires, or 48%. Their data resulted in a report called *The Work Week of a Pastor*, which deals with the workload, time management, and days off. As we look at the stressors that ministers must deal with, congregational expectations and role definition are clearly items to consider.

The average pastor is forty-seven and a half years old, works fifty-five hours a week, and handles sixteen different tasks, from administration and sermon preparation to training leaders and counseling. This survey indicated that the pastor "will spend four evenings in ministry activities and he'll take four phone calls at home after 6 PM" (p. 4). "Sixty-one percent of pastors said they would like to spend less time with administration and budget activities and preparing for and attending meetings" (p. 10). The same chart reveals that pastors would like to give less time to mediating conflict (37%), and counseling (34%). These activities are seen as less productive and perhaps more difficult for some ministers.

Managing workload and expectations appears to vary with the pastors' previous work experience. Thirty-nine percent of pastors came to the pastorate from another career, and seventy-three percent of those worked more hours in ministry than in their previous career (CRR, 1997, p. 8).

As in any job or profession, there are employer expectations and specific requirements for the employee. As caregivers in a Christian community, pastors have a variety of role expectations to perform in their function as shepherd. In the 1997 survey by Leadership Journal, their data indicated the following with relation to job requirements:

- Forty-eight percent of pastors received a job description.
- Thirty percent of pastors were provided with their churches' expectations.

35

Finishing Well

- Of these thirty percent, sixty-two percent said their actual workload had exceeded their churches' expectations.
- Thirty-eight percent of all pastors said their actual workload had exceeded their own expectations.
- Only thirty-one percent of churches provided a structured review to discuss their pastor's workloads.

It would appear that developing job descriptions for pastoral leadership and clearly identifying church expectations with structured reviews could assist both clergy and congregations in understanding the issues of workload and stress. When 36% of pastors sense an unspoken pressure to "make it appear as though they are busier than what they really are" (CRR, 1997, p. 16), it is time to clearly identify role expectations. Twenty-two percent of all pastors have been terminated at some time, and of these, 46% said they felt pressure to be busier than they really were. Pastors working less than fifty hours a week were at higher risk of being terminated by the church. It appears that congregational expectations for pastors include long hours. This author's own survey in the Assemblies of God (Wolyniak, 2004) indicates that nineteen percent of pastors have faced a forced exit, agreeing closely with the national average of twenty-two percent. It would only be fair and appropriate for governing boards to discuss openly with their ministers their particular reasons for these long hours and the quality of ministry on a frequent basis. Both pastor and congregation need to be evaluating from the same perspective using clearly defined job descriptions and reviews.

The workload of pastors is better understood when we find that the number one reason (68%) pastors think they are working too much is "they expect too much of themselves" (CRR, 1997, p.16). The second reason was there is too much work left undone, with 64% responding. Forty-nine percent of pastors have feelings of resentment for working too much. When we look at these statistics, the question that comes to mind is, where do these feelings surface in a minister's life? Even though there is resentment in a large portion of pastors for heavy workloads, only 34% consider taking a less-demanding position in ministry (p. 19). Only eighteen percent of all ministers are dissatisfied with their current workload, and that is reflected as well in the broader "thirty-one percent of all pastors who are dissatisfied with their salary as it relates to their workload" (p. 19).

4- Top Stressors of Ministers Today

The Leadership survey on workload correlates the time in ministry with physical stress, with 59% of respondents saying they had physical stress on a monthly or more frequent basis (p. 21).

Because of the nature of the Leadership Survey on Workload, we are quoting the following topic in its entirety:

Who are the most stressed-out pastors?

Those feeling stress on a daily basis are working a median of sixty-two hours per week. Those feeling stress weekly are working a median of fifty-six hours per week. The median for all pastors is fifty-five hours.

- Their actual workload has exceeded their church's expectations.
- Their actual workload has exceeded their own expectations.
- Their church does not provide a structured review for them to discuss their workload.
- They feel resentful more frequently that some church members perceive their workload as light.
- They are more likely to feel as though they are evaluated more by the number of hours they work than by their job performance.
- They are more likely to have experienced conflict with their church board, senior pastor, or other church leader regarding their workload and/or schedule.
- They are more likely to think they are working too much.
- They are more likely to feel guilty about not working hard enough and more likely to feel guilty about working too hard.
- They are more likely to feel resentful about working too much.
- It bothers them that as a pastor their job is never finished.
- They frequently wish they had a Monday-Friday, 9 AM to 5 PM work schedule with weekends off.
- They are more likely to be dissatisfied with their current workload.
- Their spouse is more likely to complain about their work schedule and their work schedule is more likely to cause conflict with their spouse.

Finishing Well

- Their children are more likely to complain about their work schedule and their work schedule is more likely to cause conflict with their children.
- They are more likely to have had their stress cause or heighten health problems.
- They feel emotional stress more frequently because of the nature of their work.
- They take their work home with them mentally or emotionally, more frequently than other pastors do, and more frequently than their first two to three years in ministry.
- They probably make a to-do list more frequently.
- They feel pressure from uncompleted tasks more frequently.
- They are more likely to take only one day or less off each week.
- They are more likely to work on their day off (CRR, 1997, p. 21-22).

The above conclusions by Leadership give a good indication of the perceptions of pastors on the causes of their stress load and the results of the stress. Life is complex and the pastorate even more so as the caregiver enters the lives of so many and on so many different fronts. It is a most taxing profession and calling, and the wise person will learn to not only manage their stress load, but also lean heavily on the grace and love of God.

In a first reading of this list of stressed-out pastors, it appears that they are doing more and enjoying it less, and the effects of this stress show up in resentment, mental and emotional turmoil, and frustration. The issue of job clarity and management are several areas that need to be discussed. The issues of a pastor's time management were also a part of the Leadership survey.

When we look at the job description and expectations in any profession, it falls on the worker to learn to manage their time to accomplish the job requirements. Although being a pastor is spiritual ministry, there is still the need to manage the limited time one has to accomplish given goals or to meet needs. There are several items that ministers can use to assist them in time management, which include time logs, tools such as day-timers and calendars, and for some, a secretary who assists in this administrative detail.

4- Top Stressors of Ministers Today

In the 1997 Church Research Report survey, 84% of pastors make a to-do list (p. 24). Those making a daily to-do list are 46%, increasing to 56% for those working sixty hours or more per week. Those working harder are keeping track of their workload.

Those pastors who have kept a log of their time at some point in their ministry were 74%, but only 23% gave it to their church and that on a very uneven basis (p.24). Those working more than sixty-five hours a week were most likely to report to their churches a time-log of activities.

Sixty-two percent of the respondents used time management tools like calendars and Day-timers or organizers. Although the data reported do not indicate it, it would be of interest to know what percentage of those pastors who keep good time management practices also feel extreme stress over uncompleted tasks. The data does show some 59% of pastors feel the pressure of uncompleted tasks weekly or daily. Only 43% of pastors have had training in time management, be it in seminars (25%), seminary or college (23%), or other sources. That leaves 57% who have had not personal time management training. Perhaps it is time for some to learn how to manage that most precious commodity, time itself.

Related to time management are the vacations and days off that are allotted to a minister. The median number of days off per week was 1.4 (p. 26), with 56% of churches only allowing one day off per week. Only 7% of pastors take two days off per week. What is remarkable is the fact that 43% of pastors usually or always work on their day off! (p. 26). That day off was normally Monday (36%) or Friday (24%). It appears that pastors are driven people, who cannot say no, and who have a strong sense of completing tasks.

When it comes to assisting pastors with times of refreshment or respite, only sixteen percent of churches offered a sabbatical, with an average of ten days. More and more churches and big corporations are offering sabbaticals as a way to retain their workers and to encourage them to establish balanced lifestyles.

Finishing Well

Summary of the Leadership Survey, 1997.

The twenty-eight page report of the *Work Week of a Pastor* (CRR, 1997), gives a good indication of the complex issues that come with the pastorate. As we have seen, clergy stress is related to workload and expectations. Management of the time a pastor has would be a first priority, as would be clarifying job expectations and recognizing the limits of a human being, also known as a pastor. Being human is to recognize limits in all areas of one's life. Churches, governing boards, and ministers must work together to safeguard the personal life of its clergy and to meet the ever-demanding expectations of their congregations and communities. The Leadership Survey can be obtained on a subscription basis from Christianity Today.

Summary of "How Pastors Rate as Leaders" Survey, 2003

Another survey from 2003 was conducted by Leadership magazine's Market Research Department. This study looked at the calling, spiritual gifts, and leadership style in a report, "How Pastors Rate As Leaders" (Reed and Hanson, 2003). This fifty-four page report utilized 168 pastoral returns out of 399 mailed for a 42% return rate, and in addition, poled church congregants of the pastor with 1,338 returns out of a possible 9,925, or 13%. The complete report may be obtained on a subscription basis from Christianity Today.

It is not the intent of this book to review all of the data and to try to interpret it. We leave that for others to pursue. Our interest lies in the need to try to correlate this recent survey with our subject of ministerial health in general, and to attempt to isolate key issues that lead to stress and burnout, as well as those that contribute to a very positive approach to pastoral health. These surveys reveal much about current conditions from the perspectives of the congregants and their pastors.

Calling and Its Perceptions

Jesus could face opposition, ridicule, persecution, and eventually death on the cross, because He was confident of the will of

4- Top Stressors of Ministers Today

God. The example of Christ is set before every believer and every minister of the Gospel. Christ Jesus is our best model for ministry, for He stayed focused on His mission.

In the previous chapter on the special call of God, we discovered that there is indeed a dynamic call that is both spiritual and yet leads to practical living for one called of God. The 2003 Survey by Leadership (Reed, 2003) indicated that 97% of pastors of congregations with less than 100 members believe they have a clear call to ministry, versus 88% of pastors of churches with more than 100 members (p. 9). Also, we must note that pastors with more than 20 years in the ministry say, "God has clearly communicated their purpose to them versus pastors in ministry for less than 20 years (91% versus 77%)" (p. 7). The issue of call to ministry is a key component for pastoral longevity and health. Defining the call and purpose of the church and its ministries will only serve to strengthen the leadership of the pastor. If church life is nothing more than a social group built around similar interests and pursuits, it loses its vitality. "More pastors from smaller churches (less than 100) than pastors from larger churches said their calling was defined by events, a 75% versus 53% (p. 15).This may indicate that pastors of larger churches see calling as a gradual process. The overall was 62% of all pastors related their calling to specific events and 37% to more of a process or gradual call.

A question that has come to this writer's attention is, "Does God call people to ministry and then gift them, or does He gift people and then call them?" Perhaps it is a little of both. The 2003 Survey indicated that 67% of pastors believe their calling uses their natural talents and abilities, with 22% or one fifth, stating that they are asked to do things they are not naturally gifted to do (p. 10). It has been taught for years that a man's gift makes a way for him. However, we have also seen God take ordinary people like the apostles and use them mightily for the expansion of His Kingdom. We must be careful at this point that we do not equate usefulness with natural ability, as God is not limited to what we bring to the equation of ministry. Ministers truly need to be men approved by God, rightly dividing the Word of truth.

Defining the call to ministry as a profession or vocation is one thing, but to work it out in everyday life is the challenge of our obedience and submission. There is a large gap of 20% between those older pastors over 50 who said, "Their calling has not changed, but the way they fulfill their calling has changed", and those under 50 who say it has not changed (69% versus 49%). It may mean that older pastors have had to adapt more to changing times and their pastoral role than the younger generation of ministers. Having experienced more of life as a pastor, older clergy members may relate their obedience to God in a more varied climate of ministerial roles. It is encouraging to see the results of this survey and the strong basis for a call to ministry.

Now about Spiritual Gifts

If God has indeed called men and women to ministry and the larger community of believers, then we should expect an impartation of relevant spiritual gifts for that ministry role. The New Testament lists a variety of spiritual gifts ranging from apostleship and leadership roles (Eph. 4:11) to more charismatic gifts such as healing, prophecy, and wisdom (1 Cor. 12). Gordon Fee makes a summary comment on First Corinthians 12:11 in relation to the diversity of gifts that God gave to His Church:

> The participial phrase 'distributing to each person' picks up the noun translated 'different kinds of' in vv.4-6, emphasizing here both the variety and the active work of the Spirit in apportioning out to the many these manifestations. Only the final clause is new: 'just as He determines', which in this context might best be translated, 'just as He sees fit' (or pleases). The emphasis is less on the Spirit's deliberation in action as on His sovereignty in distributing the gifts, or perhaps in manifesting Himself. Thus the gifts, even though they are 'given' to 'each person', are ultimately expressions of the Spirit's own sovereign action in the life of the believer and the community as a whole (1987, p. 599).

The Bible clearly shows us that there is to be a diversity of gifts in the Church, and this involves the ministers and their calling for the

4- Top Stressors of Ministers Today

building up of the body of Christ. (See also Romans 12:3-8; 1 Corinthians 12: 4-11, 28; Ephesians 4:11.)

In the 2003 Survey, most pastors and congregants agreed that pastors have the gift of teaching (Reed, 2003, p. 3). It was of great interest to notice that more pastors believed they had the gift of exhortation, administration, shepherding, teaching, or prophecy than did their congregants. In other words, pastors thought they were good at administration (42%) but their own members thought otherwise with 26%.

The Leadership Survey of 2003 noted on a chart (p.17) on spiritual gifts, that pastors and congregants think the pastor has the gift of teacher, shepherd, administrator, and exhorter, but their member's viewpoint is at least 10% less sure. The study also observed that a significant 68% of pastors believe their spiritual gift is being used all of the time, with another 27% most of the time.

It appears from the above data on spiritual gifts alone that the majority of pastors are working in the pastorate with their spiritual gifts engaged and active. This is good news for both the pastor and his people. To be able to do what you are wired for is a healthy job attribute and it decreases the stress on that part of the ministry experience.

Where does stress occur?

Stress occurs when there are expectations of either the leader or the church body or its individual membership. Stress can occur and will occur even in the best match of pastor and congregation. We are concerned for the health of both the congregation and pastor and for longevity in ministry. If pastors know and understand their leadership style and ways of management, then they can adjust and adapt to the demands that come to their office door in a more understanding way. Genuine Christian love accepts people and groups as they are and works with the Holy Spirit to make changes. Rather than being forceful or stiff, the wise pastor will be sensitive to the needs of the body and trust the Lord for direction and strength.

In McIntosh's book, *One Size Doesn't Fit All* (1999), the author states that "we cannot cause growth; we can only create a climate in which growth can take place" (p. 142). This identifies a

Finishing Well

crucial task of pastoral leadership in nurturing and developing others for the Lord to use in His kingdom work. The growth and maturing is the work of God. In First Corinthians 3:6, Paul says "I planted, Apollos watered, but God gave the increase", once again identifying where the power lies - in God alone. If one takes steps to implement this strategy, then there should be less stress on the participant's lives, as God enables them and sustains His work and workers.

Focus On the Family Pastoral Care Reports

Dr. James Dobson, Founder and President of Focus on the Family, started this ministry to attend to the needs of the family in America. In so doing, he soon realized that if families were to be healthy and growing, then their churches and pastors needed help. As a parachurch organization, Focus on the Family comes alongside leadership in a supportive role. H.B. London, Vice-President of the Church and Clergy Department, has given his time and attention to the ministers of the American church. This department has a call line for pastors and their families in need of counsel, prayer, and encouragement. The department also has a data base of professional licensed counselors and retreat centers for referrals for ministers.

In an interview with John Barner (Barner, 2004), of the Church and Clergy Department, it was discovered from six consecutive monthly Care Reports, with 1,397 phone calls, that the major concerns of ministers and spouses were as follows:

1. Marital Concerns   16.52%
2. Resources requested   13.93
3. Church Concerns   10.86
4. Child-parent Issues   9.26
5. Prayer   8.95
6. Church Conflict   6.65
7. Career   5.89
8. Referrals   5.43
9. Pornography   5.20
10. Scriptural Advice   4.44
11. Depression   3.83
12. Finance   2.45
13. Sexual Misconduct   1.99

4- Top Stressors of Ministers Today

14. Accountability 1.84
15. Forced Terminations 1.53
16. Health 0.77
17. Health/Chaplains/Sabbath 0.46

The top five concerns can be looked at as family-related, combining marital and child-parent issues; and church-related, combining church concerns and church conflict.

Here is how the above list would look if we combined a few related items:
1. Family (Marital & Child-parent)   = 25.78 %
2. Church (Church Concerns & Church Conflict) = 17.51%
3. Resources (Requests for materials)   = 13.93%
4. Prayer   = 9.95%
5. Sexual (Pornography & Sexual misconduct) = 7.19%

There are many ways of using this basic data to interpret the concerns of pastors and wives. The connecting links between these issues should be considered when reviewing the data. (Focus records that 60% of all calls were from men and 40% were from women.)

In discussing the trends in pastoral calls, John Barner mentioned that ministers are more likely to discuss these issues with a neutral party, not related to denominations or governing boards. This author asked if interpersonal conflict was one of the top issues of stress in ministry. Barner replied that this was definitely an area of stress reflected in the high numbers of calls related to church concerns and church conflict. It was also mentioned that there seemed to be more calls coming in on the subject of forced terminations where boards were acting from more of a business mindset when goals, be it finances or people, were not met.

The pastorate today is under heavy pressure due to the expectations and demands of the congregants, as well as the need to maintain personal spiritual and mental health. Leading a congregation today is not a place for the weak of heart, but it is a place whereby the power of the Holy Spirit, life, joy, and maturity are offered as a way of life for both leaders and followers in the body of Christ. A wise man develops skills in the area of interpersonal relationships for a lasting and satisfying ministry.

Finishing Well

Barner suggested that there were other related issues that need consideration if one is to finish well. He felt that a desire for life-long learning would keep pastors current in their mental work of ministry. Developing trusting friendships and support systems; being flexible with one's culture and congregants; developing a listening approach to life; and a degree of vulnerability were all listed as crucial elements of a healthy life. Team spirit and enhanced cooperative working relationships with others are also key areas for ministers to work on personally. Controlling jealousy and a competitive spirit among peers was one area that Barner felt needed discussion, as this attitude is self-defeating, and if left unchecked, can create bitterness and spiritual dryness.

The Author's Survey Results from Assembly of God Ministers

As a part of this study, the author sent out a questionnaire to thirty senior pastors in Colorado. Questions in the survey focused on five areas of ministry life. Sixteen surveys were received. The data collected helped to verify if some of the national numbers dealing with pastoral stress and ministerial health are also found in the fellowship of the Assemblies of God. The full results of this survey are in Appendix B and C.

One item that was noted was the opinion that previous Bible school or seminary training did not adequately prepare individuals for conflicts in pastoral care. Sixty-three percent of pastors said their theological training did not prepare them for the conflicts in ministry, and sixty-nine percent did not receive adequate training in conflict resolution and management (Wolyniak, 2004). Sixty-nine percent of pastors were handling stress poorly, and 43% did not feel they received adequate training in human relations. A national survey by the Lutheran Church-Missouri Synod, conducted by Alan C. Klass' company, Mission Growth Ministries, found that 40% of that denomination's pastors were experiencing mild to severe burnout (Klauss, 2002, p.1).

Churches and denominations have not always seen pastoral health as one of their key functions and responsibilities. It has normally been the personal responsibility of each minister to care for his or her own soul and spiritual health. Perhaps some have seen

4- Top Stressors of Ministers Today

ministers as strong, gifted individuals who can do no wrong, and always seem to have the answers. As we know, there are no such saints. We all have feet of clay and are in need of redemption and cleansing, as well as guidance and strength from the Lord and His Word. In the last two decades, "member care" has been a new topic as it relates to ensuring that ministers receive adequate attention and care, with growing accountability and strengthened relationships.

Caregivers can suffer from fatigue; frontal or oblique attacks on their personal character; or from being primary targets in spiritual battles as representatives of the Lord Jesus Christ. Ministers proclaim, teach, and apply the Word of God to situations in the lives of their parish or church, and this, too, can cause extra stress and conflict when the intended recipients are reluctant to follow the advice or admonitions of the pastor.

George Barna, president of Barna Research, made the following comments on a 2001 Survey, which add perspective to the statistics.

> To appreciate the contribution made by pastors, you have to understand their world and the challenges they face. Our studies show that churchgoers expect their pastor to juggle an average of 16 major tasks. That is a recipe for failure - nobody can handle the wide range of responsibilities that people expect pastors to master. We find that effective pastors not only love the people to whom God allows them to minister, but also provide firm, visionary leadership and then delegate responsibilities and resources to trained believers. Ultimately, the only way a pastor can succeed in ministry is to create a team of gifted and compatible believers who work together in loving people and pursuing a commonly held vision. The pastor who strives to meet everyone's demands and tries to keep everyone happy is guaranteed to fail (Barna, 2001 Survey, Internet source).

The researcher also noted that many pastors are not given an adequate opportunity to shine.

Finishing Well

Our work has found that the typical pastor has his or her greatest ministry impact at a church in years five through fourteen of their pastorate. Unfortunately, we also know that the average pastor lasts only five years at a church - forfeiting the fruit of their investment in the church they've pastored. In our fast turnaround society where we demand overnight results and consider everyone expendable and everything disposable, we may be shortchanging pastors - and the congregations they oversee - by prematurely terminating their tenure (Barna, 2001 Survey).

Some ministers have a higher threshold of emotional pain than others, or a different worldview by which they manage to operate within the midst of ministerial duties. Given the variety of personalities and backgrounds of those engaged in ministry, there are bound to be setbacks, differences, and conflicts when trying to lead and administer any congregation.

Missionary Member Care

William Taylor (1997), discusses the attrition of foreign missionaries and identifies four 'acceptable' reasons: normal retirement; issues related to children; a legitimate change of job; or health problems (p.10). The text goes on to study the stewardship issues related to these specially called people in the area of member care. "According to WEF's recent findings, one missionary in six (16%) never completed the first term" (p. 278). Not only do missionaries have the same stressors as their stateside counterparts, but also have the added complexity of cross-cultural issues like isolation, language, political turmoil and uncertainty, and the spiritual and personal issues of living in a foreign land. There is a lengthy time of preparation for the field, which should include the evaluations and training necessary to ensure that the candidate is ready for the field.

Member care has been defined by Kelly O'Donnell as "the ongoing investment of resources by mission agencies, churches, and mission service organizations for the nurture and development of missionary personnel" (Taylor, 1997, p. 287). Sending agencies recognize their responsibility to support the worker that they send out

4- Top Stressors of Ministers Today

and that includes more than just the financial partnership. Agencies and para-church ministries are well aware of the need to strengthen and come alongside those ministers and their families in unique cross-cultural settings. The survey listed 26 reasons why missionaries leave the field (p.175). Team reasons made up for 8% of all attrition. Learning to get along with others and possessing good communication skills are two areas that can be enhanced on the sending side of the equation.

One study by Sung-Sam Kang (Taylor, 1997, p. 251) recorded that for new sending countries, 80% of attrition was due to inadequate pastoral care and supervision of those missionaries. There is a growing awareness of the need for stronger support for workers in these types of ministry outreaches. As a former foreign missionary in a restricted access country, we were concerned with the type of support we would have on the field. It appears that no matter where ministry is taking place, be it in the local church or on foreign soil, there is a need to assist ministers and their families with appropriate care and supervision. The issue of attrition due to stress is not an American issue, for it crosses cultures and is prevalent in other ministries worldwide.

Summary

When taken as a whole, clergy are maintaining efforts to meet ever-increasing demands on their time and talents at a cost of marital peace and personal stress. The stress is present in any occupation, and even more so with the caring professions. Church life for the pastor has an abundance of sources that can cause stress and burnout. A few items do come to the foreground from the review of surveys and books on these issues.

The Bible speaks about one body with many parts, and states that each member is valuable to the whole body. Learning to work together for the common good and health of all is a primary objective in the body of Christ. The Church is a living organism and as such has needs that must be met if it is to survive and thrive. Comfort, healing, nourishment, rest, and relationships with others are just a few areas that need attention for stability and growth to occur in the minister as well as the congregation.

Finishing Well

The Austin Presbyterian Theological Seminary's Clergy Burnout Survey (Jinkins, 2002, p. 3) asked the question: How often do the following situations create stress in your life? Here is the order of the most stressed areas. We have combined the category of 'very often' and 'often'; for example: seventy-four percent of pastors believe that too many demands on their time occur 'very often' or 'often'.

1. Too many demands on my time. 74%
2. Feeling drained in fulfilling my functions to the congregation. 47%
3. Conflicting or ambiguous expectations of my work. 36%
4. Personal or family situations. 33%
5. Inadequate compensation or finances. 30%
6. Feelings of powerlessness in my work. 28%
7. Criticism of me or what I have done. 11%

You will note that there is a large gap between feelings of powerlessness in work (28%), and criticism (11%), the next ranking stress area. It appears that the top six are responsible for much of the stress created in pastoral ministry.

Interpersonal Conflict

Any list of the top stressors for pastors will be incomplete and general at best, as all individuals and specific churches will have their own culture and environment that is unique to them. What research has uncovered is that one of the primary stressors is the interpersonal conflicts between pastors and the members. This type of emotionally-laden conflict has a tendency to inhibit positive relationships. Given several of these ongoing conflicted relationships, the caregiver-shepherd can feel the strain and tension, with resulting effects on one's person, family, and further ministry. These conflicts in the church can occur over differences in vision, strategy, personality, leadership style, and a host of other items. The Alban Institute article in *Congregations Journal* (Klauss, 2002, p. 4) noted that from talking with a group of 15 pastors who had taken the Austin Seminary survey:

4- Top Stressors of Ministers Today

Their (pastors) larger concern was the personal toll that interpersonal conflict takes over time on their energy levels, on their enthusiasm for ministry, and on their love for their congregations. They spoke of being worn down by the emotional damage of interpersonal problems with their congregations. One pastor likened it to the incessant drip, drip, drip of water torture.

These pastors also spoke of the "small betrayals of trust, the corrosive influences of malicious gossip and backbiting, the apathy and despair in declining congregations, the thoughtless and snide remarks, the passive-aggressive digs among members and staff" (Klauss, 2002, p.4). It appears it is the little foxes that spoil the vine - the small undercurrents that come from the interpersonal relationships of a community church. It was interesting to observe that only one of the 15 pastors (6%), spoke of wanting to leave their current congregations. The remainder were very excited and committed to the future of their ministry and were upbeat about their calling.

Conflict can also occur from counseling others with its resulting transference and overload. There is often a reluctance to talk about feelings as they relate to interpersonal relationships. Handling the stress of intense relationships on deeply personal issues that include topics like AIDS, health, sexual issues, marriage, conflicts, and crises in members' lives, can all add up to deep interpersonal conflicts with the people under one's care.

The Austin Survey (Jinkins, 2002) reveals that 21% of its pastors felt drained of energy very often, and another 26% who were often feeling drained, for a total of 47%. These numbers are indicative of the stress in ministry life.

Marital Conflict and Family Issues

Marital conflict in a pastor's life, as reflected in the number of phone calls to the Pastoral Care Center of Focus on the Family, may well be the result of ministry pressures on the family and couple. Pastors who spend more time with the members of their flock than with their spouse and children have set the scene for conflict. A minister's marriage can be healthy and peaceful if the demands of ministry life are balanced. The Austin survey (Jinkins, 2002) showed that personal or family situations were often thought about by 33% of the participants. The Focus Survey (2004) revealed that the number one reason for pastoral calls to their ministry office was marital conflict. The stress that is a part of ministry can also find its way into the minister's own home and marriage, resulting in tension and conflicted relationships. Priorities need to be made to safeguard the minister's family from undue stress, anxiety, and burnout by appropriate scheduling, and by living out a balanced lifestyle.

Time Demands

When pastors are engaged in sixteen different activities on a regular basis, the issue of time management becomes critical. From the survey results of Leadership 2003, it appears that congregants view their pastors as poor time managers. There is a need to focus attention on better management and utilization of time. That may mean more delegation, training others, or just saying no to some of the demands, requests, and expectations of others.

The Austin Seminary Survey (Jinkins, 2002) reveals that 74% of respondents thought that there were too many demands on their time. An article in *Congregations Journal* (Klauss, 2002, p. 3) reported that the time crunch was created in part due to the fact that pastors "felt incompetent in determining priorities among the competing values and ideals that guide their ministries, and that they were unable to distinguish between goal setting with reference to their congregational ministries and goal setting in their own professional and personal lives." Pastors are in need of help when it comes to managing time and people.

Associated with time demands are the expectations of congregations for their clergy and clergy families.

Expectations of Clergy and Congregants

God calls pastors to work with the people in a local setting in a spirit of Christian love and servant-hood. Some pastors appear to be overwhelmed at the needs presented by their congregations. Pastors by definition are generalists, dealing with issues like hospitalization and sickness, to death and dying, to helping families in conflict or

4- Top Stressors of Ministers Today

crisis. Role designation and job descriptions, as well as reviews, can assist in this area.

Thirty-six percent of the Austin study group (Jinkins, 2002) often had thoughts on the conflicting expectations of their ministry workload. In general, the expectations were most conflicting from the ministers themselves. Pastors are hardest on themselves, and this creates stress and burnout.

Leadership Style and Personality

The issues of leadership style enter into the stress level of pastors. The 2003 survey by Leadership indicates that congregation's assessments of their pastors are quite different from what their pastors see as their styles of leadership. When we approach this topic, it is well to keep in mind the variety of styles of leadership, as well as the types of congregations and their general and specific makeup. Oswald and Kroeger (1988), in *Personality Type and Religious Leadership,* "believe that there are few who can bring excellence to all the functions of ministry demanded by congregations" (p.27). These authors look at the Myers-Briggs Type Indicator as a tool to help ministers understand their leadership style and personality as they relate to the complex issues of leading and pastoring a congregation.

In an article in Christianity Today (Barna, 2003) entitled "Pastoring or Leading?" the writer stated:

> Last year, researcher George Barna concluded that by contemporary models of leadership, a significant number of pastors are not leaders. Barna said 92 percent of Protestant ministers consider themselves leaders, though less than two-thirds of those pastors actually possess leadership skills. 'This research does not criticize the heart or ministry of pastors; it simply affirms that they will have their most positive effect through the exercise of other gifts and offices,' Barna told a pastors' group. 'Pastors are good people, well-educated and called to ministry, but perhaps not to the ministry of leadership' (Barna, 2003,p.1).

Finishing Well

Stress and conflict are inevitable when pastors are seen as shepherds and not leaders. To know oneself is critical to a lasting and joyful ministry life, for both the pastor and his family, as well as those to whom they are called to serve. Reed and Hanson (2003) said that the results of their survey with Christianity Today for Leadership Magazine indicate that:

> The longer a pastor stays with a congregation, the more likely he is to see himself as their shepherd. Only 53 percent of pastors serving at a church less than five years said shepherding was a primary spiritual gift, compared to 73 percent of ministers with longer tenures (Reed, 2003, p.3).

Knowing what our gifts are and our leadership style will do much to enhance the productivity and maturity of ministry in both the leader and their congregation.

Accountability

The Austin Presbyterian Seminary survey (Jinkins, 2002) reveals that 41% of its ministers in that fellowship had developed sufficient mentors for accountability purposes. This author's own study (Wolyniak, 2004) recorded that 31% of ministers do not have a friend they can turn to for accountability, and 43% are not reaching out to new ministers in their area.

Other studies indicate that clergy are reluctant to develop lasting relationships with their peers, especially within one's own denomination, as they want to present a strong face to other ministers and not show their weaknesses and vulnerabilities. When facilitators are present to assist in clergy care issues, ministers respond in these open, safe, and trusting relationships. A fair portion, 38%, of Assembly of God pastors would keep to themselves if they were struggling in an area of their life, with only 31% saying they would get help. These numbers suggest that ministers are reluctant to develop accountable relationships, a great source of strength and support for finishing well.

In a study entitled "Secondary Stress, Burnout, and the Clergy", the authors report that "members of the clergy are exposed to

4- Top Stressors of Ministers Today

many of the same client problems, including traumatic material, as their counterparts in the mental health profession... and reported experiencing emotional and physical strain associated with these client contacts and a few required professional help themselves" (Holoday, 2001, p. 66). There is opportunity for the client's stressful situation to become stress for the clergy who is offering a listening ear and a caring heart. Caregivers need friends, others in ministry-related professions, and prayer to stay healthy. A major concern for the directors of the study was that too often clergy did not have accessible support systems, as does the mental health worker, with supervision and accountability. Clergy who had dual relationships as pastors and therapists "may have more continual exposure to parishioners-client's traumatic or stressful experiences than other therapists" (Holoday, 2001, p .68). For most clergy, counseling is a scripture based process of help, and is often practiced without the parameters or limits that professionally trained counselors employ. The study went on to discuss coping strategies for secondary stress for clergy involved in counseling. This is an accountability issue on a professional and spiritual level.

    The reasons for stress and burnout in the ministry are many. There is sufficient data from a variety of sources, surveys, and books that acknowledge the results of stress for pastors and their families. Diagnosis of the problems inherent in a ministry environment is fairly easy as we see the results of stress and burnout all the time. Developing solutions to maintaining spiritual health for clergy are available with the help of caregivers, friends, ministry support groups, and the Lord Himself.

CHAPTER 5

A THREEFOLD CORD

There are three areas that need review in the process of helping one to stay strong and to finish well the task of ministry. These are the dimensions of our personhood or being which include character, competency, and commitment. This threefold group of topics sets the tone of ministry life and will determine how well one accomplishes God-given tasks and assignments. When these three are in agreement with scripture and the spirit of Christian living, then we can pursue the other areas that need strengthening. These three answer the questions: Who am I? What do I have to offer? What is my passion and commitment? Ecclesiastes 4:12 states this basis for a foundation: "And if one prevail against him, two shall withstand him; and a threefold cord is not quickly broken." Our strength for the journey is found in Christ.

Character and the Minister

Who we are as human beings comes before who we are as ministers, pastors, or missionaries. As people for whom redemption in Christ has become a reality and living relationship, there are now areas of our lives that need constant attention and self-care for our gifts and purposes to be utilized and realized. The first issue is that of character development and its relationship to ministry effectiveness. The character of a person directly influences competency and success in ministry.

How is character developed?

More than the ability to minister is the character of a person that is most valued by God. Within the calling to minister is the call to holiness and integrity on which ministry is based. Character is the inner workings of the person, and is developed over time by the experiences of life and our responses to them. Character is born in the midst of life's often harsh realities. It is in the midst of the difficulties

Finishing Well

of life - the family of origin, misfortunes, or the results of our own choices - that our character, our true personhood, stands out. There are books and studies of psychology and sociology that deal with the issues of character development. We want to look at a few issues of character that relate to ministers and leadership.

One's spiritual formation and maintenance of that personal life that is hidden from view develops over one's lifetime. Bible study, prayer, reflection, worship, and meditation all are used by God to develop our spiritual life and have a profound impact on our character development. We must be like Timothy who was told to "Do your best to present yourself to God as one approved, a workman who does not need to be ashamed, and who correctly handles the word of truth" (2 Tim. 2:15).

Family of origin, and the experiences we had when we were young, all contribute to who we are and how we see our world. We thank God for the power of Christ to transform us and conform us to His likeness. We do not need to stay in this world in a broken, or abused condition, but can find reconciliation and redemption as God restores us to a right standing in Christ. People are known for what they do, and how they act in public. At the heart of this observation is the knowledge that our actions are a result of what we believe and think, and in many ways how we faced the issues of life before this present moment.

Character establishes and determines ones destiny. Without strong spiritual character, one jeopardizes ministry potential. Failures in ministry are normally not a result of poor management, or the lack of dynamic preaching, but flaws in one's character (Stowell, 1997, p. 113). Clinton believes that many leaders become frustrated in the early years of ministry because "they do not recognize God is working *in* the leader and not *through* him or her" (Clinton, 1988, p. 46). The impatience of youth brings about many a failure to finish the task of ministry.

When it comes to the issue of personhood as it relates to why some people fail or fall into sinful habits, Stowell says there can be a "fatal flaw in their personhood that has given the adversary an opportunity to accomplish subterfuge and to either discount or debilitate their capacity to lead" (Stowell, 1997, p. 113). When we develop a strong spiritual foundation, a spiritual formation, we place

5 – A Threefold Cord

safeguards around us that can withstand the attacks of the enemy. Maintaining spiritual vitality, spiritual disciplines, and a fresh relationship with Christ will do much to ensure a strong sense of personhood. Those who have fallen from their high calling in Christ are usually found to be wanting in maturity and development of Christian character and values. Those who have fallen have not maintained the hidden life of Christian character development. God is more concerned about our character than He is our comfort. This is probably why we grow most in depth of character in the everyday realities that at times test us, and try our spirit. We grow more in adversity than easy prosperity. David had the strength of character to say "Search me, O God, and know my heart; test me and know my anxious thoughts. See if there is any offensive way in me, and lead me in the way everlasting" (Psalms 139:23-24). When we seek God's face, He will come to our aid. Eighty-six percent of pastors in one study said their top priority is their personal relationship with God (The Parsonage, 2001).

Charisma without character leads to chaos. One can be a dynamic personality with the favor of man, but can end in disgrace and disaster if one's character is not Christ-focused and grounded. Charisma, according to Drucker (2001, p.269), becomes more of a problem than a blessing. It makes them inflexible, convinced of their own infallibility, and unable to change. Drucker takes a stand that neither charisma nor a set of personality traits makes a leader. Effective leadership is "thinking through the organization's mission, defining it, and establishing it, clearly and visibly. The leader sets the goals; sets the priorities; and sets and maintains the standards" (p. 270). From a Christian point of view, who the leader is as a person rightly related to Christ and how he expresses himself in word and deed is more valuable than great accomplishments in ministry or attainments to some denominational leadership role. The person in ministry is valued by Christ more than the ministry. Recall the incident in Luke 10, where the disciples came back rejoicing over success in casting out demons and the miracles that attended the preaching of the Word of God. Jesus said, "However, do not rejoice that the spirits submit to you, but rejoice that your names are written in heaven" (Luke 10:20). Jesus clearly wanted the disciples to understand that the eternal value of a person was based on a relationship with Himself, and not in performance or duty in society or church life.

The leader's character and stability is more valued than charisma alone. We only need to look at a few characters in the Old Testament - Saul and David for example - to see the outworking of a weak character trait. Saul, for all his charisma and physical stature, was found as one whose heart was spiritually weak and whose ego was so strong. Saul fell from grace long before he fell in relation to his kingship role (1 Sam. 10:1; 13:8-14; 15:10). We find King David wanting in the area of maintaining his spiritual values when he fell for Bathsheba and sinned in the area of adultery and murder, (1 Sam. 11-12), the consequences of which were to plague his life and those who would follow. So we are cautioned to maintain our character even if we have a natural flair or gift of charisma with people. Making wise choices on a daily basis is what character is all about, and not just in the big moments. What we do in the daily small moments and decisions of life is a good indicator of spiritual health.

How is character maintained?

Being comes before doing. What we believe results in actions. Character leads to conduct and conduct reveals character. Scripture is replete with admonitions and imperatives instructing us how to live our lives for Christ. The Apostle Paul instructed the believers at Thessalonica how to live their lives:

> Finally, brothers, we instructed you how to live in order to please God, as in fact you are living. Now we ask you and urge you in the Lord Jesus to do this more and more. For you know what instructions we gave you by the authority of the Lord Jesus. It is God's will that you should be sanctified: that you should avoid sexual immorality; that each of you should learn to control his own body in a way that is holy and honorable, not in passionate lust like the heathen, who do not know God; and that in this matter no one should wrong his brother or take advantage of him. The Lord will punish men for all such sins, as we have already told you and warned you. For God did not call us to be impure, but to live a holy life.

5 – A Threefold Cord

Therefore, he who rejects this instruction does not reject man, but God, who gives you His Holy Spirit (1 Thess. 4:1-8).

Without holiness no man shall see God. What we are and how we live in purity of life is more important than our success rate of winning souls or managing a fine church. Holiness is not an option for the man and woman of God in a leadership position. Maintaining holiness requires us to be self-disciplined and reflective on our thoughts and actions. Putting off the old man is the beginning of salvation, but putting on the new man, clothed in the righteousness of Christ, is a process that continues for a lifetime.

One needs to be a follower of Christ before one can lead others to Christ. When we let down our standard, or our love of Christ in obedient faith, and succumb to the easier way of drifting, then we lose our footing, our foundation, and we are likely to fall. At a minimum, we will most likely fail to achieve the goals for which Christ originally called us. Gravity has a strong and natural pull on our bodies and the world and its allures has the same effect. One needs to be aware of, and willing to withstand, the downward pull of spiritual compromise with the world's attitudes, and to take a stand for Christ by developing a strong spiritual character. Character development is honed in the battles of life; in the inner working of the Spirit; and in the outgrowth of a strong prayer life. In his book, *Born For Battle*, R. Arthur Matthews (1978), states that " this is not the time for God's soldiers to withdraw into passivity, to put reality out of their minds…it takes conflict and the fact of an enemy to put prayer in perspective as a significant factor in furthering the cause of Christ in the world" (p.10). Conflict will come into our lives to test our character, to test our spirit, and to allow us an opportunity to rise up to the occasion for the cause of Christ and His Gospel. We must align ourselves with the gospel and the power of Christ if we are to finish well in life.

Self-discipline comes before disciple-making or even dissemination of the truth of God's word. When one learns the ways of the Lord from experience, then they are in a better position to lead others in the way of Christ. The inner life growth process develops one's character in the early stages of leadership development and growing maturity.

Finishing Well

Stowell (1997) reviews the passage in First Timothy 4 and lists five qualities for ministers to develop: speech, conduct, love, faith, and purity (p. 125). These are areas that will need constant attention and safeguarding against the erosion of faith or the attack of the enemy of our souls.

God chooses to use people who are committed to Him and making progress in their lives. (Stowell, 1997). Those who would be most effective have deep consistent spiritual character, a life of integrity that leads to respect, and a track record of progress. Integrity comes from a word group that means whole, or complete. We are to be always growing, learning, and striving to attain both the knowledge of the Lord and His Word. Our lives need to be whole, in what we do and express, as well as what we believe deeply. A divided life will only end in chaos. God calls us to maintain a spiritual vitality that overflows to others in ministry. A minister's life should exemplify Christ at all levels, and this takes constant vigilance.

Strong biblical character in a minister is essential as a model for others to follow. If one is lacking some of the basic Christian character traits, their life will affect, if not infect, those around them. No one is perfect, but we all need to be in the process of conforming to the image of Christ and His nature. Transformation of our heart and our worldview takes place on a daily basis as we make choices that either reflect the love of Christ or deny that love.

Respect as a Value to be Earned

When ministers live lives of faith and integrity at all levels, then there is a healthy life that can be respected and looked up to by the congregants. "If a shepherd has obvious gaps in his integrity, respect will soon be undermined. It's difficult to respect someone you cannot trust" (Stowell, 1997, p. 107). Stowell talks about integrity issues related to keeping confidences; how one approaches relationships; and faithfulness to one's spouse and people in general. If ministry is to have the respect of the congregation and the larger community, then it has to be earned as never before. The failings of a few diminish the view that people have of those who remain in ministry. We need to live up to the claims of Christ on our life if we are to impact others for eternity.

5 – A Threefold Cord

It used to be that ministers were thought of highly, along with the local physician. Now it is not uncommon to see and hear degrading remarks about ministers or churches, all due to a few who let down their guard or whose true character was revealed. In the absence of Christian character, the voice and message we hear is a shallow word among us. The truth of the message of Christ remains strong, but its messengers have at times fallen short of representing Christ in their character. The failings of the messenger call into question their submission and obedience to Christ and His Word. An old saying comes to mind, "Preach the gospel by all means, and if necessary, use words." Our lives are to be living epistles read and known by all men. We are admonished throughout the Bible to be an example in speech, and in life itself.

As a witness for the Lord, we must admit that in some ways Christianity is on trial in our own lives. People are watching us, and especially those who promote the gospel as His representatives in leadership roles. Let us live up to the claims that we preach, teach, and share, so that others can see Christ in us, the hope of glory.

There is a deep need for ministers to have moral purity and a purity of motive for doing ministry (Stowell, 1994). The issues of moral purity deal with the physical arena, whereas motive has to do with the real reasons one does ministry. Both issues stem from attitude of the heart and spirit and affect the leadership ministry. Strong self-discipline and a commitment to purity of thought, word, and deed, as well as the right desires for doing ministry bring the blessing of the Lord. A weakness in this area eventually shows up in one's life and ministry. Motive questions need to be asked and addressed all along the path of ministry life. Why do we do ministry? Is it for the rewards, the money, the esteem, or for the glory of God? For what purpose do we do what we do? Who are we trying to impress? Do we do ministry as unto the Lord or for the praise of man? When we honestly answer these types of questions, we can root out a spirit of pride, rebellion, or jealousy, and come to grips with the changes we need to make in our inner lives.

Finishing Well

Attitude Is a Choice We All Make

"Attitude is a choice and I am responsible for it." (John Maxwell, interview on TV, PBS, on Joyce Meyers, October 5, 2004). "I am responsible *to* people but not *for* people." If ministers take this outlook on their ministry responsibility to people, it will defuse another potential stressor in feeling responsible for other peoples' choices and lives. We are engaged in the everyday lives of people we love, but are not responsible for their choices or the results that proceed from them.

Attitude is one of the prime issues of character development that affects ministry. Ministers need to continue to develop and maintain positive attitudes in both their calling and the outworking of that call in relationships. Ministry has great blessings and great sorrows. Ministry tasks call for individuals who are strong mentally, emotionally, and spiritually. An attitude that is positive, upbeat, and encouraging will bless any congregation.

Spiritual Disciplines

The process of spiritual formation includes the disciplines of reading and studying the Word of God, meditation on Spirit-taught truths, prayer, Sabbath keeping, participation in worship and praise, keeping accountable in relationships, and learning to be led by the Holy Spirit. We undermine our own calling when we fail in these critical areas.

One's true character is revealed in the midst of life's leveling lessons. What we do when we don't get our way often shows our inner character. How one responds to disappointing news, or how one behaves in a crisis, reveals the inner workings of one's value system, and in the end establish who they really are. What we claim to be, what our words may even say, pale in comparison with what we do with our lives in moments of testing and trial. The old saying that 'actions speak louder than words' is really a maxim that speaks about one's character. "It is not failure that makes or breaks a person, but how he responds to it. If he can learn from his failures; if he can persist in spite of failure; if he can maintain a positive attitude, a forward look, then he will succeed in life no matter how many times

5 – A Threefold Cord

he fails" (Exley, 1995, p.150). A similar thought is made in *Mid-Course Correction* when the author looks at the disciple's reaction to the feeding of the five thousand. "The character of a person is revealed in how he responds in moments of impossibility" (MacDonald, 2000, p. 191).

Character alone will not assure a good finish. We must be committed to a life based on biblical values and spiritual insight into the Word of God, as well as submission to the teachings of the Spirit. When it comes to developing godly character, there is no better place to start than with scripture, which instructs us and can bring discipline to our souls. Paul wrote in Second Timothy 3:16, "All scripture is God-breathed and is useful for teaching, rebuking, correcting, and training in righteousness, so that the man of God may be thoroughly equipped for every good work." It is a lifetime commitment to the very word of God that will keep our mind and spirits attuned to the mind of Christ.

When Christ called the fishermen to follow Him, their journey would result in their individual character being tested, tried, and purified. God would transform this group of unlikely men into His anointed apostles. With the coming of the Holy Spirit in their lives, God took who they were, with all their personality traits, and transformed them into agents of change in a very secular and pagan society. As they surrendered to the leading of the Lord, they found that His grace was sufficient for them at every occasion.

Everyone has a character, a personhood element to their lives. It is when they have surrendered to the Lordship of Christ that it becomes sanctified. The process of character development continues throughout the life of a believer. We are ever being challenged to surrender a jealous spirit, a deceptive attitude, or a critical evaluation of others to the Lord, and come to grips with allowing the Lord to change us for His glory.

Character Counts

Character is more valuable than productivity, charisma, or social skills. Character is what we are on the inside and what makes or breaks us in ministry. Men and women who are in the role and

Finishing Well

position of pastor and leader need to have a character that is Christ-honoring. Warren Wiersbe said that "no amount of reputation can substitute for character" (Wiersbe, 1980, p. 81-82).

It was once said by a senior pastor that "God is in the business of transforming our character to be like His." Leaders today are especially under the microscope of review by society and their own parishioners when it comes to character and the qualities that are expected of a minister in the work of the Lord. May those in leadership roles in Christian ministries truly be found in possession of, and in the growth process of, qualities of greatness that come from the throne of God. Truly we are to 'imitate Christ' in all our relationships and in our pilgrimage.

There is a great theme verse for life that is found in Psalms 84:5 that points to the attitude in regards to this area of character development and the journey of a spiritual life. "Blessed are those whose strength is in you, who have set their hearts on pilgrimage".

Know Yourself

To know and understand who you are and what you have to offer in the area of gifts or skills is an important part of finding joy and satisfaction in ministry. When we work outside of our skill level or giftings, there is a better chance of dissatisfaction and even depression, let alone perhaps doing a job poorly. There is a vast array of materials on leadership, spiritual gifts, and assessments for one to explore. We will look at this topic in a later chapter.

As with all professions, it is easy for the minister to become so familiar with their duties and role that the activities they are engaged in develop into a routine done with little thought or feeling. When this second nature relationship develops, the minister can foster more of a professional life than one of calling and depth of character. It is essential that spiritual disciplines be maintained for the Christian pastor. A healthy living and loving relationship with Jesus Christ must be evident and nourished or burnout is sure to occur. We cannot assume we can do the work of the Spirit in the energy of the flesh and accomplish what God has planned.

It is not unusual for a person to be intellectually sound in their theology of the faith and yet lack the heart relationship with the

5 – A Threefold Cord

Founder of the faith. Hands and Fehr, (1993), in discussing intimacy with God, state that "what is missing in such a life is a deeply lived love relationship to the One about whom this person speaks" (p. 55). Too often clergy and laypersons have a performance based lifestyle rather than one focused on the love, affirmation, and appreciation for who they are in Christ. There is within the church a certain push or drive to activity, often to the exclusion of a healthy relationship with God. A close loving relationship with Christ is absolutely necessary for the works of the church to be blessed. Just as faith without works is dead, so too works without faith is dead. Faith must come first and then works of faith should naturally follow.

How does a person come to the place where they recognize their need of God's love and grace? It is usually when we are humbled by some event or action of our lives that we recognize our need of God's grace and forgiveness. Our pride will keep us from coming to the Lord, but a humble heart will open the windows of heaven itself. Jesus said, "Blessed are the poor in spirit, for theirs is the kingdom of heaven" (Matt: 5:3). Healing and grace come to us when we are willing to admit our need to God and others. This is an ongoing process in relationship to the Lord. The surrender of our control issues is not a one time event, but a daily dying to ourselves so that the love and grace of God might be given out as well as received. John the Baptist said, "He must increase but I must decrease" (John 3:30).

It is easy to overlook our own spiritual condition when we are so involved in the lives of others. When we will honestly take a spiritual inventory of our lives, we can then see our need of God, and make the necessary adjustments to get back in relationship with Him. There is a call for renewal and rest, as well as growth, in the matters of the heart. Many ministers, suffering from burnout due to stress, lack a healthy relationship with God on a personal level. Their role as minister or missionary can be harmful to their own spiritual journey if they neglect the issues of the heart.

Personal Conflicted Lives

Clinical research by Hands and Feyr (1993) indicates that the vast majority of clergy persons who have gone to the renewal center

Finishing Well

in Wisconsin had addictions at some level that affected their lives and ministry. These substance abuse or compulsive behaviors were found to be used as a way of escape from the burdens and stress of ministry or interpersonal unresolved conflicts. Pastors are people who face the issues of life, and who are also trying to function in a care-giving role. The healers often need healing, and that comes by maintaining an open and robust faith relationship with the Lord on a personal level.

One ministry director, Artis Miller of Freedom Ministries, in an interview (2001) acknowledged that there is a very high percentage of clergy clients who are wounded leaders who have developed unhealthy practices as a result of not dealing with the personal issues of their lives. They carry with them into ministry the private pain of rejection, abuse, and unresolved conflicts with the resulting fruit of bitterness, anger, and resentment. All these negative emotions and feelings adversely affect minister and ministry alike, and unless they are confessed and dealt with, they will hinder the move of the Spirit. As ministers have similar needs, wants and desires, there is a place for transparency and openness to God and others, so that there develops a balance between the public and private life, between giving and receiving, and between being and doing. We are first of all called to be a child of God, and then called to some particular work or ministry.

Spiritual Dangers for Clergy

What are the potential dangers that exist for the one called of God to a life of ministry and outreach? There are several that come to the top of the list, including a spirit of professionalism and image management to those in the public world; intellectualism versus humility; giving but not receiving; development of addictions and compulsive behaviors due to the stress load; and inappropriate behavior between the sexes due to irrational thinking or a lack of discipline. These are some of the issues that come to mind as we look to find solutions and governing principles that can assist and encourage those in pastoral leadership roles.

Hands and Feyr (1993) suggest that there are three spiritual dangers for clergy: the empty cup; saying and not doing; and escapism when burdens become too heavy (p. 59). Each of these possesses the capability to affect the minister adversely.

<u>5 – A Threefold Cord</u>

Developing Competency Skills for Ministry

As much as one wants to be used of God in ministry, one needs some level of skill or ability to minister. We are valued by God for who we are - His children - and not by performance or productivity. The world view of our culture is to produce, achieve, overcome, and master our environment, whereas the Christian view is to be obedient in humble faith to the leading of the Lord and to His Holy Word. Service comes out of a life grounded in Christ. Having been accepted in the beloved, we now serve Him and others as a result of our acceptance. Ministers are no less prone to forget that they are valued, regardless of what they may or may not do. God would have us as a redeemed people doing works of service and ministry as an outgrowth of the inner life relationship. The old saying, "saved to serve", has driven many a person to a life of performance, rather than one of grace and being led by the Spirit.

When it comes to the order of work and ability, faith comes first, then works of faith. Ephesians 2:10 says that we "are God's workmanship, created in Christ Jesus to do good works, which God prepared in advance for us to do".

Typically, competence - the ability to do things well - comes with time and experience. We acknowledge that God has gifted each person with a variety of spiritual as well as natural abilities. One should focus on their strengths or giftings and build a ministry on those. To neglect areas of weakness would be wrong, but to spend an inordinate amount of time and energy in this area could be counterproductive. We do not have all the gifts needed for ministry, but we do have a few. Just as Paul reminded Timothy to study to show himself approved of God, we are reminded that we are to be pro-active in managing our gifts and improving our understanding and skill levels.

One of the foundational truths found in scripture is Ephesians 6:10, which says we are to strengthen ourselves. Self-discipline in the Word and in the Spirit is a continual and active process and is dependent on the individual alone. We see this truth expressed in Luke 4, where Jesus is led by the Spirit into the desert. The temptation episode concludes with Jesus being victorious, as He had secured the knowledge of the Word of God and was led by the Spirit. This was

Finishing Well

not presumption, but preparation of the life that would be our example.

Competency in the Work of the Lord

Competency, the ability to perform or accomplish a task, is necessary for any ministry to take place. Many skills can be learned over time. With an attitude that says, "I can do this", blessings come to those in need, and people are encouraged in their lives. A great variety of abilities are necessary in the role of pastoral leadership. Just because a person wants to be a pastor, or to preach or teach, does not necessarily mean they have the gift. Although we would admire anyone who wants to do a task, there must be some basic ability to perform in that area, or we have a disaster in the making. Competency can be a natural ability or gift, and with a right attitude, bring the desired blessing to others. Competency can also be enhanced by training, by application of new principles, and by experience. Ministers need to be intentional and pro-active to maintain and improve skills in ministry.

How to Develop Competency

Ministers are faced with a large job portfolio that includes a variety of diverse and challenging tasks. John MacArthur (1995, p. 290-296), gives seven practical requirements for Christian leaders that are the main essentials of effective leadership:

1. A good leader manages himself.
2. Knows how to make good decisions.
3. Communicates effectively.
4. Manages his leadership style.
5. Gets along with people.
6. Is able to inspire others.
7. Is willing to pay the price.

Competency in any area of ministry can be improved by finding a mentor or coach who can come alongside and share their insight and wisdom. One denomination now assigns a mentor to each

5 – A Threefold Cord

ordination candidate for a nine-month period. This mentor has specific items to address during these monthly meetings. In an effort to assist these local pastors, the mentoring program is a requirement for ordination. So far, there have been very healthy responses from the candidates. A full description of the Mentoring Program of the Rocky Mountain District Council of the Assemblies of God can be found in the Appendix. Although mentoring is normally seen as a long-term relationship, mentoring in this case has a closure and specific goals set by the District and the protégé.

Coaching clinics and Boot Camps are now a very popular and productive way to encourage both new church-planting pastors as well as revitalizing pastors of older congregations. Attending one such clinic, this author went away with a new appreciation for the need to share thoughts and ideas with others in more of an "ask; don't tell" mode of communication. It was refreshing to find that coaches of pastors can impact others and bring dreams to reality by being active participants in a relational setting.

We can learn new ways of leading and guiding. Innovation, and energy combined, result in new ways of doing ministry, of reaching out, or of solving problems. Competency does come with time and experience, but some skills can be jump-started when we apply ourselves with a deep commitment to seeing the body of Christ grow healthy and strong.

Success and health in ministry are related to the issues of commitment to the call and the competency to perform various tasks. When there is clarity of the task to which we are called, then one can search out ways to accomplish those ministry-related tasks. Applying oneself to finding out the answers to difficult theological or interpersonal issues is a basic component of effective and efficient work skills.

Competency and skills may be enhanced by theological education and practical seminars and training. True competency, the ability to do a certain job, is polished, refined, and re-defined in the everyday workplace of ministry. It is on-the-job experience that develops competency as one relates to others and learns to recognize the changes that may need to occur to do a more efficient and effective job of ministry.

Finishing Well

God has given each person unique individual strengths, and it is these strengths, gifts, abilities, and empowerments of the Spirit on which a leader should focus for improved ministry effectiveness. Too often, we concentrate on improving our weaknesses in a skill area, only to find that our improvement is marginal. Better to give time and energy to our areas of strength and delegate the other responsibilities to more capable people.

Strive to be a Lifelong Learner

Peter Drucker (2001) states that in a knowledge society such as our American culture, there is a need for continual learning and re-learning to keep abreast of the changing times. "One implication of this (in an entrepreneurial society) is that individuals will increasingly have to take responsibility for their own self-development and for their own careers" (p. 325). If that is true of the business world where the bottom line is money and security, it is also true of the Christian in his faith walk. Self-discipline and a desire to be a life-long learner in the things of God and how they relate to society will strengthen the believer and be a witness to a skeptical society.

Social and communication skills can all be enhanced by attending seminars. Books, tapes, or CD's can also assist a minister to develop new skills and understanding of a variety of subjects. Continued education, adult learning, and night schools all offer a variety of subjects to broaden one's horizons and connect them with very useful information that may apply to ministry life.

Too many ministers have quit learning the ways of the Lord and His Word, and coast on old knowledge and experiences. We need to be life-long learners, ever eager to search out the Word of God, to inquire, to investigate, and perhaps to reshape our own understanding. Growth is a purposeful, intentional event. It doesn't just happen. Being intentional in our study time, our prayer life, our private and public life, will bring us to the attitude of heart that says, "Here I am, Lord, use me." The life that is committed to strengthening one's understanding and investing in one's competency level will enlarge the borders of one's influence. God will use all that we bring to Him when we are focused on bringing Him glory through what He has placed in our lives.

5 – A Threefold Cord

Build on Your Strengths

Being an effective leader requires many things - character and competence being just two of them. Tom Demarco (2001) in his book *Slack*, said, "You're efficient when you do something with minimum waste; and you're effective when you're doing the right something. It's possible to be one without the other: efficient but not effective, or effective but not efficient" (p. 122). Doing the right thing that God has given us to do with the help of the Spirit, enables efficient management and the carrying out of God-given tasks and responsibilities.

Peter Drucker (2001) in a chapter entitled 'Know Your Strengths and Values', discusses the essential need of individuals to know where they belong. By answering three questions: what are my strengths; how do I perform; and what are my values; one should be able to decide where he or she belongs (p. 224). Christian ministers need to learn who they are and come to a place where they can manage themselves to make the largest contribution to society. Drucker sees the management of self as the key to success and satisfaction in a world bent on more productivity in quantity and quality. The ministry of Christ should be done by individuals who have disciplined themselves to a life of biblical values that show up in the marketplace and not just on Sunday morning.

Commitment and the Minister

The commitment to a ministry is based on the commitment to the essential and initial call of God upon a person's life. The joy and excitement of being used by God, to be entrusted with the greatest news given to humanity, is to be in love with Christ and the people to which He has called us. Over time, through the hardships and difficulties that come with leadership, it is easy to lose sight of the One who called us in the first place. There are several issues related to a strong commitment to the call and to the work: cultivating a servant/shepherd attitude; strength of character to stay in the work in the midst of difficulties or lack of observable results; and commitment to one's core values.

Finishing Well

Cultivating a Servant Heart

How we serve others as a shepherd needs to measured by the example of Christ. "Though He had a high position, in fact the highest position in the universe, He was willing to use that position as a platform from which He could serve. Pastoring is not a pedestal. Pastoring is a platform from which we minister to the flock on His behalf" (Stowell, 1997, p.134). A pastor is an undershepherd of Jesus Christ, and as such is given authority and opportunity to impact people for Christ. Any other reason for wanting to be in a position of leadership needs to be surrendered to the Lordship of Christ.

The attitude that remains committed to the Lord will carry us through the hard times of ministry life. If we are committed, we will be secure and confident that God will undertake for us in areas of weakness, fears, and concerns. Only as we put our trust, and with it our actions, in the Lord's hands, will we be steady and able to help others know His loving care and provision.

If we are not committed to the Lord above all others, then we will most likely vacillate between staying in the midst of the storm, and moving on. Commitment to the call of God, to that initial and growing awareness of His touch on our lives, will keep us when all other claims on our lives fail.

Commitment and Security

Commitment is an essential of leadership. If one is to have followers, then one must be committed to the relationships and the focus of that ministry. Without commitment there is no security. We will always be looking elsewhere, over the next hill, horizon, or community. Ministers need to be committed to the Lord and His call and the task at hand; otherwise, a lack of commitment will show up in both job performance and personal relationships. No marriage, business, or community effort will last without a commitment by its members to one another.

Commitment says it is willing to maintain a work ethic and relationship even when things are not going according to one's

5 – A Threefold Cord

expectations or vision statements. The real test of one's commitment is in the trials, tests, and constantly changing environment of life. The reality test of life with its pressures and mounting stress reveals our true heart commitment. It is at this point that what we believe or say we believe is tested, and a time of evaluation is made to either adjust our values and beliefs, or hold tight and stand firm. Starting out in ministry for most was a time of high idealism and expectations of what could be. As time goes on, many only see what is, and lose the hope and dream of God meeting with people, including the pastor.

Committed to a Lifestyle of Hope

Developing a lifestyle of hope with positive returns for one's investment of time, energy, prayer, and life itself is necessary for both the leader and the people. We must come back to the fact that "unless the Lord builds the house, we labor in vain that build it" (Zech. 4:6). Knowing that we are co-laborers with the Lord - that it is His work and He has called us to it - allows us to join God on the journey of faith and work alongside Him. It is easy to get side-tracked into thinking that it is all up to us. Ministry takes place when we follow the Lord in obedient faith, and rely on His strength in the midst of our weakness.

Commitment to the Lord Jesus Christ, with no strings attached, releases us to be ourselves for God. Too many are comparing themselves with themselves and the scripture says that they are not wise (2 Cor. 10:12). By believing that God has both called us and stationed us in a location to accomplish His plans for the people among us releases us to let God lead the way. The opposite is to think that we are here working for the Lord and asking the Lord to bless our efforts. The Lord Almighty has called us and equipped us and desires that we trust Him for the results and strength to accomplish any degree of ministry success. Commitment to hope, that spiritual ingredient which makes life more than what we see, and more than what we generally expect, is what we must strive for.

Finishing Well

The Test of One's Commitment is in Relationships

Ministers face this reality test of life in the complex outworking of relationships within the community of believers. The intimate pastoral relationships that typically grow between pastor and people will test the commitment the pastor has made to his calling and his people. The outworking of how to fulfill the vision and mission of a congregation will inevitably cause conflicted relationships between the pastor and his people. A wise shepherd will find support from within that fellowship and in private prayer and other relationships. A commitment to the kingdom view of ministry must replace the smaller and often myopic view of one's personal expectations of how ministry is to occur. The shepherd needs to develop a larger view for the good of all.

The commitment of the leader must consider the needs and expectations of his followers, and either win them over in the course of time, or find new people who will join his vision and eventually outnumber those whose voice is currently opposed to possible change. Commitment to the long-term vision, with an understanding of short-term issues, will assist the pastor in the long term. Finishing well means one is committed to doing what is right, fair, and spiritual for the congregation. To finish well, one needs to be committed to maintaining their hope in Christ, that God will indeed bless the precious moments of grace between parishioners and pastor at critical times in their lives. It means that as a pastor, one does not give up on people, tough circumstances, or when there is a lack of growth in numbers or finances. Ministry is more than a business approach to organizational management. We must get back to the fact that church life and congregational issues are part and parcel of living for God, and that pastoring is more than finances, growth in numbers, or program development. Pastoring is taking care of God's people; standing with them; believing with them and in them; encouraging, equipping, and loving them. This type of kingdom commitment is a joyous adventure even in a very complex and modern world. God still rewards those servants who minister the presence of Christ during a family's loss or dark times. God still honors those who are committed to staying the course.

5 – A Threefold Cord

This type of spiritual commitment is not born in the halls of academia, or obtained upon ordination, but is birthed in the quiet times of one's devotional life. Active faith does not stay in the work of ministry just for the good times and accolades of man, but is a seasoned faith which sees beyond the stress, the strain, and the pain of living. It knows that God will bless every effort, every touch, every kind word, every cold glass of water to a thirsty soul. God, as King of the kingdom, will reward all those who serve with an undivided heart.

Divisions of the heart in the area of commitment occur when we begin to take our eyes off Jesus. When the strain and burden of shepherding people becomes more of a responsibility and less of an opportunity, it can, and often does, become a routine job. The minister in this position needs to see that we labor for the Lord; that it is work that takes a toll on us; and that only God in Christ can renew our strength. "They that wait upon the Lord shall renew their strength; they shall mount up with wings as eagles; they shall run and not be weary; they shall walk and not faint." (Isaiah 41:30)

The enemy of our soul can take advantage of a weakened leader who has borne the heat of the day. Rather than defending the defenseless, the hireling runs when the wolf comes. The commitment was shallow, essentially a job to be done, with little ownership or sense of obligation. There are those in ministry today and in the past who basically found ministry as a good place to make a living. This author has met a few men who, when talking about ministry, actually stated that "ministry is a great way to make a living", and they had in mind the perks and position of authority that came with the pastorate. There was a shallow commitment to the kingdom view of life. Their lives had become routine in dealing with the lives and needs of people, rather than passionate.

Passion for the Work and for the Lord of the Work

Without passion for the work and for the Lord, all our efforts and plans, if not covered in prayer with a sense of awe and dependency on God, end in wooden forms of success. Commitment to Christ and His work should be exemplified by a passion for souls, for the heart to be heavy for people's losses, and excited and joyous in their victories. When we are driven by the love of God in our ministry

Finishing Well

tasks, then we will sense the joy of the Master as well as the love of the people we serve. Those who are half-hearted, performing the duties but distant from people, will eventually be found out. It should be said of us by others, "Behold, how they love one another." This is not an option; it is a critical area of leadership strength.

Commitment is listed here as one of the most important areas of strength or weakness in a leader's life. In church ministry, those who would lead others must be followers of Christ. Commitment to doing what is right, spiritual, and even costly at times, will go far to see people strengthened in their faith and encouraged in their journey. With less commitment, one is more likely to look for shortcuts to success, which may bypass waiting on God in prayer, or the patient endurance which is honored by God. Longevity in ministry requires a second wind in the seeming marathon race over the long haul.

Commitment has strong links to character development. Without a "stay at the task" kind of resolve, we can soon stray to easier avenues of service or just become lazy in ministerial tasks. Commitment says : "I am a man of my word. I will do what I said I would do. I will finish the job. I will not give up in prayer or hope for people or circumstances. I will continue being faithful, not just in public, but in private, for I know that God will reward not only me, but those to whom I have been assigned to minister Christ and His love."

Jesus shows us commitment, in that He could have called ten thousand angels to get off the cross of Calvary. It was not the nails that kept Jesus on the cross, but His love for all of humanity that kept Him there. He submitted to, and was committed to, pleasing the Father. As Redeemer of mankind, Jesus' commitment was evidenced in the Garden when He prayed, "Not my will, but Yours be done." He submitted to the larger kingdom purpose of eternal life for those who ould believe in His name. Jesus is our supreme example of commitment.

If our commitment to Christ and to the call of God remains consistent, we can expect our lives to be both productive in the eyes of God and rewarding. The effect of strong commitment and dedication to our calling brings with it a security and sense of well-being that only God can give us. The birth of a church in the heart of a pastor is an exciting adventure of faith, and it takes a spiritual

5 – A Threefold Cord

commitment to see that dream fulfilled and realized. Often a great work outlives its love relationship, and in time, one's first love is lost. Programs, rituals and treasured traditions may continue on and outlive the purpose and passion that the group once possessed. (London, *Heart of a Great Pastor*, 1994). Commitment to loving Christ and others is a primary target for our energy and efforts.

Over-Commitment to the Work

Although statistics show that pastors are often found to be working more than a forty-hour week, it is not because they are forced to do so, but because they are a caring and committed people group. Their commitment to the people in their lives reveals a holy regard for the calling and outworking of that call in the involvement in peoples' lives. There is great reward and blessing to be involved in so many lives for the Lord, and to find the help of the Spirit for each and every need. God's goodness is expressed in that those He calls, He equips and keeps. God is committed to His people and to His shepherds (1 Thess. 5:24).

A clear Christian commitment involves us all, both leader and people. When we make a decision to follow the Lord, to love Him and His people, to pray for the lost and to do our part, it really means we will continue in that pursuit of truth and righteous living, even when the going gets tough. Commitment is what keeps our marriages together, our families strong, and our churches operating. There are times when things are not easy, or enjoyable, and perhaps more routine than romantic. That is where commitment is tested. That is where the minister needs to stand strong in his call and firm on the knowledge that his Lord who called him will also enable and supply all his needs. Hosea 6:3 states this blessing: "Let us acknowledge the

Lord; let us press on to acknowledge Him. As surely as the sun rises, He will appear. He will come to us like the winter rain, like the spring rains that water the earth."

Finishing Well

Summary

The threefold cord of character, competency, and commitment establish the leader within the realm of spiritual calling and giftings. It is up to the Spirit of God to bring them all together as the surrendered leader finds empowerment for a lasting ministry.

Establishing a strong foundation in these areas with the leading of the Lord and submission to His will opens doors by the power of Christ to fulfill one's calling. When we do not understand who we are, then it is more difficult to see how God could use us for the ministry demands that are around us. Congregations need loving, qualified, and committed individuals to minister to their families the Word of God. The example the minister offers by his life is the most valued component of ministry.

CHAPTER 6
STYLE OF LEADERSHIP

Leadership Defined

Those in pastoral leadership often struggle with their shepherd's heart for people and the need to give vibrant and visionary direction. Most models from the business world seem rigid or awkward and might not be transferable to the local church and ministry setting.

There are as many definitions of leadership as there are those speaking to the topic. A good definition comes from George Barna, in *"A Fish Out of Water" (2002)*. He said leadership is "the process of motivating, mobilizing, resourcing, and directing people to passionately and strategically pursue a vision from God that a group jointly embraces". When we think about the variety of personalities, ways of relating, and objectives of ministry leadership, there arises a need to identify one's own personal style.

Leadership in the body of Christ calls for special skills, calling, and understanding of this often complex issue. The gift of leadership is listed in Romans 12:8 as one of many gifts that Christ has given the church. When ministers and ministry teams and staff apply themselves to finding their place in leading the body of Christ, then they are well on their way to fulfilling their call.

Wilkes (1998) makes a clear distinction between natural giftedness for leadership and the spiritual giftedness that comes from God with empowerment to lead. Many who have natural abilities to lead are not always able to lead in spiritual matters. One only has to look at King Saul who totally missed God in the end. The church today and its pastors need to clearly identify what a Christian spiritual leader looks like by biblical example and standards; otherwise, we become like the world and lose the power of Christ to transform lives and society.

Finishing Well

Max Depree says that "the first responsibility of the leader is to define reality" (Wilkes, 1999, p. 64). To explain the future as one sees it, clearly and with grace, leaves no doubt in the follower's mind what leadership sees as their vision and mission. Vision is what the mission looks like when it is finished.

The sons of Issachar (1 Chron.12:32) knew the times and the seasons in which they lived and they knew what to do. They were perceptive of present conditions which brought information and awareness, and then they were knowledgeable enough to know what to do with that information.

The issue of leadership authority over others is a valid consideration to understanding how to finish well in ministry and life itself. "Spiritual authority is not a goal but a byproduct. It is delegated authority that comes from God. It is the major power base of a leader who has learned God's lessons during maturity processing" (Clinton, 1988, p. 167). When we realize that the authority we have over others is a gift from God to influence them for His purposes, then we can use it to enhance, and not control, other peoples' choices and Christian maturity. The role of clergy includes the "one-way communications (sermons) that are neither challenged or questioned" (Hands & Fehr, 1993, p. 42). This sense of power over others can isolate a minister from facing the truthfulness of their lifestyle, their choices, or their inner struggles. The probability of abuse is high if a needy "narcissistic cleric meets an obviously needy and distressed parishioner who comes for help" (p. 42).

In recent years, there has been a trend away from the traditional shepherd role to that of more of a business-entrepreneurial leadership style. The effectiveness of the church is now being measured in some quarters by the business model of leadership. Barna (2001) reports that when it comes to leadership, only 4 % of pastors say they have the gift of leadership. This striking comment comes at a time when all eyes seem to be focused on bottom-line numbers, be they attendance or finances. Perhaps we are using the wrong model when we compare ministry with a business, CEO-style of relating. A more biblical and scripturally correct approach is to see, once again, that shepherds are in the nurturing, encouraging, teaching, and modeling profession, and not just managers of people. Shepherds care

6 – *Style of Leadership*

deeply about their people and are passionate about seeing them achieve victory, growth, and maturity in their lives. "As long as position is honored above discipleship, church leaders will honor the ambitious over the obedient" (Wilkes, 1998, p.71).

It is true that each minister/leader has a style of leadership that will shape the future of that local congregation, and that style needs to be understood with both its strengths and weaknesses. Effective ministry takes place when God is allowed to use the gifts He has placed in a person for His purposes. Stress occurs in leaders when they either do not understand their style of leadership or they refuse to consider other ways of assisting people. Stress and undue conflict occur when there is a poor match of pastor and people due to style of relating or style of pastoral leadership and responsibility.

Five Smooth Stones

In Chapter 5, *A Threefold Cord*, we viewed the issues of our personhood or being. Now we will look at the issues of our doing - the work-related issues that ministers deal with on an everyday basis. There are five large groupings of stressors that we will explore: Style of leadership; Time management; Accountability; Nurturing relationships; and Demands and expectations that lead to conflict. We will use the acrostic **STAND** for these five topics. As five smooth stones were collected by David for his sling prior to confronting Goliath, so we will collect some thoughts and principles help the minister finish well in his journey and ministry of faith. We, like David, will need to stand our ground, basing our life on biblical principles, and examples of godly leadership.

The issues of one's style of leadership discuss *how* we lead. The chapter on time management looks at how one utilizes the commodity of time. Accountability focuses on building support and accountable relationships. The discussion on nurturing relationships speaks about how we relate to and manage our relationships with family, friends, and peers. Looking at demands and expectations emphasizes the importance of job and ministry descriptions, and sheds light on how we manage conflicts.

The Bible is a rich depository of the lives of great leaders of the faith for us to examine. Although the principles of leadership are not recorded as such, we have examples and character studies from which we can learn. The very word leadership is *proistemi* in Greek. It is a verb meaning "to manage, direct, lead; to devote oneself".

Understanding one's own style of leadership will help eliminate stress and tension and provide a better platform for the work of ministry. The Lord not only calls men and women to a ministry, but also equips, gifts, and establishes those in leadership. Stress and burnout often occur because the minister does not know his own gifts and leadership style. Burnout may not kill you, but it will diminish the quality of life and create tension all around. Stress, on the other hand, if left unchecked, does have the potential to kill one physically. We want to understand the basics of our leadership style and how it interacts with others in organizations, small groups, and under pressure.

Giftedness

To be yourself and not try to be someone else establishes the individual in their giftings and brings a wholeness so necessary to effective ministry. Bonnie Kopp, a Women's Ministry advisor at Multnomah Bible College, relates this concept of personhood: "You simply cannot be all that God intends you to be when you are trying to be someone else. I have become convinced that one of the main causes of burnout in ministry is not working in our own areas of giftedness" (Roberts, 1999, p.180). To operate in the area where God has gifted us is to fulfill the potential which the Lord has in mind for us.

In the last several decades, there has been a plethora of books, seminars, and articles on discovering your personal spiritual gifts. The church has been blessed with a wide variety of helps to assist individuals and leaders in identifying their areas of giftings and abilities, and then to process them into ministry. It would be appropriate for pastors to take advantage of such assessments and surveys, and inquire into their own unique calling and gifts from the Holy Spirit. It has been demonstrated in local churches across the country that when a person's gifts are identified, then placement and mobilization in ministry is not only easier, but much more rewarding and fruitful. Stress is reduced when one is operating in the areas of

6 – Style of Leadership

one's passion and ability. Under the guidance of the Lord, He makes many parts function as one, each unique in their own area, yet contributing to the body as a whole. Romans 12:5-8 expresses this idea:

> Just as each of us has one body with many members, and these members do not all have the same function, so in Christ we who are many form one body, and each member belongs to all the others. We have different gifts according to the grace given us. If a man's gift is prophesying, let him use it in proportion to his faith. If it is in serving, let him serve. If it is teaching, let him teach; if it is encouraging, let him encourage; if it is contributing to the needs of others, let him give generously; if it is leadership, let him govern diligently; if it is in showing mercy, let him do it cheerfully.

The Appendix directs the reader to explore several types of surveys that may be of assistance in determining one's spiritual gifts and abilities. (Appendix E- Internet Resources).

Trust as a Key Ingredient

Demarco (2001, p. 152) believes that leaders acquire trust by giving trust. Giving trust to others in advance of demonstrated trustworthiness enhances the relationship and establishes more trust. Giving responsibilities to those around us in ministry is a risky business, but as we learn to trust people, we can entrust them with more responsibility, and in turn, gain their respect and trust as a leader.

Once a minister loses the trust of an individual, ministry to that person is minimized. Gaining trust again will take time and humility. Being aware of how one relates to people, or is perceived by people, will help one to stay balanced and perceptive about how ministry takes place. The best thing a minister can do when they have made a mistake, a poor decision, or any offense, is to confess with a repentant heart to the one offended. Being transparent, humble, and repentant endears the minister to his people. Most folks realize no one is perfect, and will grant forgiveness and grace once again.

Finishing Well

Leadership styles

Successful ministry in a local church setting is the result of a good match, or marriage, between the pastor and the congregation. Within the body of Christ, there is a broad spectrum of how church ecclesiology manages leadership placement. Some pastors are placed in a church by the governing presbytery or regional leadership. Others allow the local congregation as an autonomous body to call and elect their pastor. There are other types of church government that work in this area of administrative and leadership placement. Stress for a pastor can occur when there is a poor match of personality, style of leadership, or congregational, as well as pastoral, expectations.

The 2003 Leadership Survey, *"How Pastors Rate as Leaders"*, identified leadership styles and found that pastors see themselves primarily as shepherding and bridge-building leaders (Reed, 2003, p. 22). This report of 168 pastors and 1,338 of their congregants, gives a great perspective on the topic of style and role of the pastor within the setting of the local church. The whole issue of leadership styles is related to the way we manage to get the work done, and includes the management of people and resources, as well as interpersonal relationships.

Pastors saw themselves as using a coach/team style of leadership (35%), while their members viewed that style only 13% of the time. Congregants also differed with their pastors who said they used the teacher/student style.

Every individual has their own strengths and weaknesses, and a pastor's are more open to scrutiny, as his life is very public and vulnerable on many fronts. This study by Leadership (Reed, 2003) identifies significant differences and found pastors more likely to see themselves as analytical, adaptable, flexible, and practical, while their congregants viewed their pastors as thorough, inspiring, self-confident, and helpful. Seventy-four percent of the "congregants describe their pastor's leadership strength as enthusiastic" (p. 26).

The survey from 2003 (Reed, p.4) identified fifty percent of pastors as having said they use "shepherding" and "bridge-building" leadership styles. Four in ten pastors said their styles are "directional," "team building," and "visionary." As gifts tend to facilitate ministry, it was discovered that the gifts of teaching and

6 – Style of Leadership

shepherding were highlighted by eighty percent of pastors. Shepherding involves that typical nurturing ministry that flows from a strong personal involvement in peoples' lives. It helps the congregants mature in Christ to become active participants in the gospel outreach. The bridge-building style of leadership would seem to indicate a strong ability to build consensus and team. Those with strong relational people skills would be more likely to be represented in this category, much like the team-building concepts of George Barna, as cited below.

George Barna, of the Barna Research Group, (*New Study*, 2003), developed a Christian Leader Profile, and came up with four styles: Directing, Strategic, Team-Building, and Operational. These categories, like the personality types of the Myers-Briggs Temperament Indicator, evaluate leadership qualities and traits within the context of ministerial aptitudes, gifts, and assessments. This Profile was based on a 177-question diagnostic with a national sample of 1,344 Christian leaders. It is to be noted that determining factors in the study, such as age, position, and leadership aptitude, had an affect on the outcomes of the study.

The four leadership types or styles that the Barna Research Group develops are as follows:

The *directional* style of leadership sees the "big picture" and focuses on the vision for the future. Because these leaders are out front in the journey, they often struggle with having a loving heart and a servant attitude (Barna, *New Study*, 2003). They often tend to be aggressive, and focused on the future, which can be problematic for some people.

The *strategic* leaders are more analytical and look for options to meet objectives. These leaders are "the strongest types of leaders when it comes to a mature faith and exhibiting biblical wisdom." The downside is that they often are impatient with those of a dissimilar opinion.

The third style of leader is the *team-builder*, who works hard on discovering and mobilizing people around their gifts. These individuals are truly people-oriented and have strong relational skills.

Finishing Well

However, they often struggle in communicating their ideas or goals for the group.

The last group is the *operational* leader, who is primarily concerned with developing systems that allow the ministry activities to move along smoothly. Because of their focused attention on the process, they often are weaker in the areas of relational strength, servant-hood, and teaching ability.

Servant leaders

Regardless of the style of leadership one is accustomed to using in ministry, it needs to reflect a servant-leader heart for effective ministry. Jesus is our primary example as He modeled this servant heart in His ministry to both the apostles and people around Him. John 13 is the strongest passage that portrays Christ as a leader who humbled himself to do the work of a slave. In this passage, Jesus took the towel and basin of a slave and performed the daily mundane task of washing feet.

We see that Jesus showed the full extent of His love for the twelve. His actions spoke of a deep and dedicated love. Jesus even washed the feet of the one who was to betray Him. The humbleness of stooping at the feet of the disciples gave a vivid and lasting lesson of servant leadership.

We are commanded to wash one another's feet. This act of humility on Jesus' part showed the spirit in which genuine love should operate. Rather than expecting to be served by others, the disciples were to be humble servants, meeting others' needs, to communicate not only the message of salvation, but the spirit in which Jesus ministered. Ministry is practical in its nature. Sharing the love of Christ, the message of the gospel, and doing acts of service can win people to the Lord. Ephesians 2:8-10 suggests that God has prepared in advance works of service for His people to do after experiencing the salvation of His love.

We realize our need of being a servant of all. No servant is greater than his master. What Jesus did for his disciples, the disciples should do for others. We have here more of an example of heart-attitude, rather than an example to continue physically washing feet. The disciples were told to be servants of all, and thereby be leaders

6 – Style of Leadership

who brought the blessing of Christ to others. As ministers, we are to be looking for ways to serve others, so the kingdom of God may grow and His name be glorified.

The whole foot washing episode in John 13 reveals a loving Savior who humbled himself before mankind, so that man could rise up and serve others. What Jesus did, the example of His life and work, we as followers are to emulate and duplicate in our ministries. Leadership here is doing what needs to be done. Jesus came to serve, and to give His life a ransom for many.

Four Styles of Relating

Leadership Development by Dr. Thomas Graham (1998, p.47) identifies four types of relational styles - exhorting, edifying, enabling, and empowering. Each of these profiles describe a particular style with its corresponding commitment and skill level. Each of these is useful at some point in leading, yet a strong leader will use that which is most effective with a particular individual or team to accomplish the goal. For a leader to use only one style of leadership may hinder the development and success of the organization . When a pastor can use a variety of styles in relating to people, then their skills and abilities will be maximized. To get the best performance from people, a leader needs to know his own skills, and those of others. Leadership is a means to achieving goals.

Personality Type and Leadership Style

The Alban Institute published a book, *Personality Type and Leadership Style*, by Roy Oswald; (1988), that does a great service by opening up the theory of personality types established by Katherine Cook Briggs, and her daughter Isabel Briggs Myers, using the writings and insight of psychologist, Carl Jung.

The Myers-Briggs Type Indicator (MBTI) evaluates sixteen combinations of eight measurements of preference by individuals. This psychological instrument has allowed caregivers in a wide range of disciplines to evaluate their personality type and better understand themselves in their leadership roles. The Myers-Briggs Type Indicator is the most widely used instrument in the country for assessing

Finishing Well

personality type as it applies to leadership. (Oswald, 1988). Oswald suggests that by taking the time to learn the MBTI types, the parish pastor will become more effective in ministry to the wide range of people in his care. The MBTI instrument helps us see how we normally perceive our world and how we relate to others. The Appendix gives further information on where to obtain information about the Myers-Briggs testing material and interpretation as well as other assessment tools.

Concept of Team Leadership

The Old Testament is full of classic individual leaders like Abraham, Moses, David, and the prophets in which we can see a variety of leadership styles. Moses had Aaron and a team of elders, and David had a team of advisors, but it is the New Testament that gives us a clearer picture of team leadership. In the developing early church, it was the apostle Paul who consistently surrounded himself with others like Timothy, Titus, and Barnabas to share in ministry efforts.

The team ministry concept allows others to share their gifts in a cooperative setting. A summary statement from Gangel (1989, p.60) who quotes John Stott on the importance of team ministry says, "There is the fact that team members supplement each other, encourage each other, and thirdly, are accountable to each other. Each of these areas strengthens ministry efforts and helps the leader share responsibility in accountable relationships."

A study of Acts 6 and 13 reveals the need for a team effort and the response of the early church to establish others in ministry as a team of dedicated workers. Paul was one who enlisted others to share their spiritual gifts in the propagation of the Gospel. There is less of an *independent* attitude portrayed in scripture and more of an *interdependence* on each other that magnifies the name of Jesus Christ. Rather than superstars that shine for Christ, we see more of a team spirit that shares responsibility and interacts with each other to accomplish ministry tasks.

Wise and successful ministry leaders find, develop, and enlist others on the ministry team, and therefore increase the effectiveness of the ministry. Ministry teams and their development form a crucial

6 – Style of Leadership

part of any local church, and under wise guidance, can accomplish more for the kingdom of God than the solo approach that often prevails in churches. A group of people do not equal a team unless they have developed common goals and the willingness to work together for the growth and development of the ministry.

One of the difficulties of developing a team leadership concept is that the pastor must relinquish some control and allow others to participate with proper oversight and management. Releasing ministry to subordinates with the proper instruction, training, and ongoing encouragement, benefits all concerned. Pastors no longer have to do everything, and lay workers are now involved by participating in their area of interest and gifting.

Developing leadership in the church is the primary responsibility expressed in Second Timothy 2:2, "and the things you have heard me say in the presence of many witnesses entrust to reliable men who will also be qualified to teach others." The Spirit of God speaks to the issue of team partnership within the context of discipleship. The primary task of the church and its leadership is to encourage others to participate in sharing in the work of the Gospel.

Modeling Christ as a Leader

Modeling Christ means that a leader lives out their Christian values and beliefs which are observed by others. It is not necessarily intentional, in that one is trying to show others how to live, but is a natural process of living for Christ before others - no show intended. Observers see that the minister lives what he preaches and is faithful in the daily routines of life, family, spouse, and community. All leaders model their lives openly before people, and as people observe them, they either decide to follow and do the same things, or they choose not to follow. We all model some style and values as we live our lives. The minister's task is to model Christ for all to see. As Paul said, "Follow my example as I follow the example of Christ." (1 Cor. 11:1)

A leader is called to model the stewardship of their God-given gifts. "Stewards choose partnership over patriarchy, empowerment over dependency, and service over self-interest" (Wilkes, 1998, p.108). If leaders see themselves as stewards of these gifts and have the best interests of the church at heart, then indeed a loving ministry will take place. If one is selfish, and fearful of giving up ownership and control from an authority of position, then one will fail to see God utilize them fully. Positional authority loses its effectiveness because others may sense they are being used to accomplish the agenda and goals of the leader instead of being given authority to accomplish their own God-given goals and objectives. It can become a power struggle, in the sense that the followers may not have a voice or sense of ownership in that ministry. Modeling, and practicing the truths of God's word, including a shared responsibility, brings a team spirit to the church.

We are not to be considered as *image makers*, but *image restorers* with the help of God. When we are real, open, and honest, the truth of God gets a genuine hearing. Being transparent and genuine are keys to healthy spirituality. Elisa Morgan, president of MOPS, stated: "Vulnerability is believability and Christianity is believable when it is lived out by vulnerable Christians" (Roberts, 1999, p. 219). Modeling is not play acting. To be effective is to be called to live a life that is sacrificial in its willingness to be genuine and real, even at the cost of being misunderstood. Modeling Christ is living out the gospel at every level of relationship and involvement in such a way that the grace and love of Christ shine through us.

The Kingdom Style of Leadership

Gangel (1989) recognizes that contemporary culture sees leadership in a different light than the gospel of Jesus Christ exemplifies. Kingdom-style leadership is countercultural in that it is in our weakness that God becomes strong; it is when we give that we receive; it is in the fact that when we are last, we will be first. This upside-down kingdom is contrary to the business school approach to leadership, which looks at success as always being bigger and better, and sees successful people as those who are aggressive and can use their political clout to accomplish their purposes.

Christ's way of leadership is a humble servant attitude, willing to suffer and think of others more highly than oneself. What a difference there is in God's kingdom! The Lord has called His people *out* of this world's way of thinking and acting. A leader led by the

6 – Style of Leadership

Spirit needs to be a patient person. "You cannot be impatient and humble" (Wilkes, 1998, p.53). As followers of Christ, we are to manage our lives, our time, and our ministries in a spirit of reflective grace and love. Grace, in that we have been given this time, this calling, to serve Him; love, in that it is the quality, the motivation, the essence of being a believer in Christ. Love is the context of our message of redemption to a competitive world, shackled with sinful ways, and for whom Christ died.

Leadership that follows Christ brings people out of this world's value system that honors growth even at the cost of one's integrity. May ministry leaders see the power of Christ in action when they operate from a biblical mandate that we are *in* the world but not *of* it! Too much of the current church scene has to do with image, and with what one can get from attending a certain church, rather than focusing on a servant attitude where one comes to serve and be a blessing.

Mentoring as a Means of Leadership Enhancement

The disciples of Christ had three years of training under the Great Shepherd. Their lives were impacted by the Master as He taught, mentored, coached, and counseled. A good definition of mentoring comes from *'The Making of A Leader'* by Bobby Clinton (1988). He states:

> Mentoring refers to the process where a person (the mentor) with a serving, giving, encouraging attitude, sees a leadership potential in a still-to-be developed person (the protégé) and is able to promote or otherwise significantly influence the protégé along in the realization of potential (Clinton, 1988, p. 130).

When a person has a gifted and sensitive mentor, they can receive great encouragement, affirmation, and insight for their own ministry. Submission to the mentor requires one to be open to new ideas, to challenges to the established way of doing things, and to the possibilities of the future. Mentors bring with them a variety of gifts

Finishing Well

and expressions, much as Barnabas was a mentor to Paul in his early ministry development (Acts 9:27; 13:1, 7, 42). Paul became an apostle of greater ability and giftedness as a result of the mentoring relationship he had with Barnabas.

Leadership needs to receive mentoring from others, as well, with their advice, giving, suggestions, insight, and leadership understanding, as well as proposals for future activities. Present leadership can grow stronger and more effective when they have mentors who are gracious, and have the gifts of faith, wisdom, and exhortation. Not only do leaders need those who will invest in *them*, but they are chosen by God to invest in *others* under their own leadership and ministry. Pastoral leadership should be on the outlook for potential leaders whom they can impact for Christ by investing in them in a mentor capacity. The Paul-Timothy relationship is a New Testament example of a mentoring relationship. Paul, who was mentored by Barnabas at the foundational level, is now the mentor for Timothy and a host of others who traveled with him on his missionary journeys. By investing in these younger leaders, Paul insured that there would be capable leadership for the next generation.

Jesus, the supreme Teacher, mentored the twelve disciples during his three years of ministry. He gave himself to these men and used everyday events to teach, model, and mentor towards greater spiritual understanding of the kingdom of God, His own identity, and how to minister that truth to others. Jesus challenged, gave direction, and explained truths at those teachable moments, so that the disciples would later recall how the Spirit worked in their Master's life.

Second Timothy 2:2 establishes this style of leadership where the leader equips and trains others in the Word of God to such an extent that they are able to reproduce other leaders. The admonishments in Paul's epistles to both Timothy and Titus reveal such a mentoring relationship where Paul's advice and spiritual insight are given, and as far as we know, accepted.

Mentoring is passing along the rich experiences and insight from an older or more experienced minister to another. This element of leadership growth ensures that the lessons one generation experienced and grew stronger in will be used to quicken the maturing process of the next group of ministers and leaders.

6 – Style of Leadership

Those who would be mentors see the potential in others and invest in them, often over a long period of time. Mentors work with a few people whom they see as open to learning and committed to the task at hand. Mentoring is based on relationship alone. Most mentoring relationships are established by a person seeking the benefits of a capable mentor. Hopefully, pastors will look around them to discover potential leaders to mentor over a lifetime.

Bobb Biehl (Mentoring, 1996) says that mentoring involves the nurturing aspect of relationship development. "The definition of nurture is to promote development by providing nourishment, support, encouragement, etc., during the stages of growth" (p. 26). A mentor is usually asking, "What can I do to help you?", rather than using a structured teaching or training format. Most mentoring is done on an informal basis over a long period of time and is concerned with a holistic view of life. Unlike coaching, which applies itself to training and equipping for performance in certain areas, mentoring focuses on the whole of life - be it spiritual, personal, career, physical, or financial issues.

The gift of a mentor in a pastor's life can greatly enhance their success in ministry. As mentoring is based on the protégé's needs, questions, or issues, and not the agenda of the mentor, information and encouragement are given where there is the greatest felt need. The benefits of a good mentoring relationship, according to Biehl (1996), include having access to wider experiences and resources, a supportive relationship during hard times, and an objectivity of viewpoint that brings a clearer understanding to issues or choices at hand. Mentoring brings with it more than advice and insight; it brings a fresh and supportive relationship that grows ever deeper and stronger over time. Pastors would benefit greatly by seeking out those few individuals who would invest in their lives and share at those teachable moments in one's life.

Summary

Every leader brings with them a certain mix of gifts, talents, abilities, and personality. This package of leadership style develops over time and through a variety of people-oriented relationships and experiences. We recognize that it is God who calls, empowers, and

Finishing Well

enables leaders to use their gifts to minister. It is incumbent upon leaders to know themselves well enough to perceive their place in ministry to the body of Christ.

It is the experience of denominations and governing boards that when there is a clear definition of need, an assessment of skills and abilities available in human resources, and a focused approach to bring the two together, then there is a fruitful marriage. Each leader will approach the complex issues of managing and administrating tasks, people, and resources differently, and should be aware of their own style, strengths, and weaknesses. Unlike Jesus, who clearly knew what was in man, today's leaders need to look for other tools of assessment besides relying on their own intuition and hunches. Again, being sensitive to the Holy Spirit, and responsive to His leadings and guidance, leaders can grow and modify their styles to fit changing circumstances and needs.

The minister who would finish well in his calling would be well advised to evaluate his own style of leadership. Ascertaining if one is a strong team leader, a mentor, a modeler, or one who delegates effectively, will help define ministry outcomes. When ministry is given out from a servant heart, there is health and satisfaction for all participants.

There is nothing better than to stay fresh, optimistic, and yet challenged in what God is doing in one's ministry. The need to understand the dynamics of personality and leadership styles is evident where ministers struggle with church boards and parishioners, and where a definite 'fit' does not seem to exist. It is the wise person who will become vulnerable in the assessment process to discover their gifts, leadership style, and personality differences, and how they may need to adjust their ministry or perhaps even move on to a ministry setting that is more suitable. It is not a hard task to find out how we think, manage, and operate in one of the most difficult positions dealing with people. It is another task and challenge altogether as we open ourselves to truly hear what others are saying, what our track record has to say, and then what the Lord Himself would speak to our hearts. There is great wisdom in a multitude of counselors, and anyone who will listen, learn, and approach ministry with the mindset of a servant-leader, will find the resources and grace to make the changes necessary for more effective ministry.

6 – Style of Leadership

Discussion and Action Steps dealing with

STYLE OF LEADERSHIP

Investigative Questions to Consider

1. Do you know your personality type based on the Myers-Briggs assessment tool?

2. Are you more of a process person or a people person?

3. Is it easy for you to delegate tasks to others?

4. What do you think may be hindering the growth of your ministry? Is it possible it is your style of leadership?

5. Are you more focused on *results* of ministry, or do you enjoy the *process* of ministry? What do you think is the difference?

6. Has ministry been more about achievement than fulfillment?

7. Are you often comparing yourself to others in ministry?

8. When you lead, do people follow quickly?

9. Do your gifts match your present ministry position?

10. Are you a relaxed person, or are you on the edge all the time?

11. Are you fulfilling one of the leadership mandates of Ephesians 4:12, preparing God's people for works of service?

12. Has one of your goals been to develop more of a team concept of ministry?

Finishing Well

Action Steps

1. Take the Myers-Briggs Type Indicator for clarifying your personality type.

2. Read two new books on leadership every month.

3. Do a spiritual gifts assessment with your key leaders.

4. Take time to pray and seek God with other peer ministers.

5. Check out the concepts of leadership style online.

CHAPTER 7

TIME MANAGEMENT

One of the greatest stressors for pastors is that of not having adequate time for all the activities that make up ministry. There are demands and expectations on one's time that need clarification and prioritization. Survey results reveal that the issue of time management is of critical importance for ministry health. With a high percentage of pastors working more hours than the average congregant, there is a need to manage time more effectively. In the Leadership Journal article, *How Pastors Rate as Leaders* (2003, p.9), it is reported that "forty-six percent of pastors called time management their greatest weakness."

Historically, the expected number of working hours has changed. In today's society, workers are being paid more and working less. Ministers and their churches need to consider what is appropriate and customary for their area of pastoral care. When the average work week of a pastor is 55 hours, and the average of the church membership is 40 hours a week, then some consideration should be made, some effort to lighten the load by delegating or restructuring ministry life. The lack of longevity in ministry is often linked to the stress of too much to do and too little time or help available. It is more often a result of poor time management.

The driving factor for many pastors is that of what Jones (2001, p. 27) calls "the two great delusions." These are the ideas of indispensability and invincibility that can hinder the minister from resting in Christ. To always be on call is to create a life on the brink of fatigue. The constant demand for the time of a minister, and the call to meet pressing needs, has the potential to topple a minister's equilibrium. There are limits to what can be done, and knowing those human limitations and keeping within them can reduce stress and burnout.

Finishing Well

Evaluate How Time Is Used

We need to do the right things well. Busyness is not necessarily a sign that God is working. It may mean that the minister cannot say no to requests and activities. Being intentional, and selecting those things that are most productive and in keeping with the mission of one's call can release the pastor from the tyranny of the urgent to concentrate on what is most important. When ministers evaluate how they are gifted and called to serve, then they have come one step closer in using their time wisely. We often try to do many things well and end up doing a poor job in many areas. Choose a few and give your whole heart to them. Barna (2001) said that most people can only handle five things at one time.

Keeping a log of your use of time is the only way a person can identify the time wasters - those items that consume your days. Drucker (2001) suggests that keeping a log of your time, then pruning, delegating, and recognizing the time you may be wasting, will in the end prove beneficial. "Time is the scarcest resource, and unless it is managed, nothing else can be managed" (p. 240).

Strong leaders use time wisely and effectively. There are a number of time management tools available. Most pastors use a daily to-do list, and coordinated with a day timer, it can give direction and clarity to priority issues that need attention. Overload happens when we have too much to do. Demands by others or self-imposed can tax us quickly. A majority of pastors create their own busyness and place demands on themselves. This may have more to do with self-esteem than it does with genuine ministry.

One of the habits that traps ministers is that of procrastination. Putting off important things is both ineffective and poor stewardship. Adequate planning focuses attention on using the time available to accomplish job requirements and ministry opportunities. To do the truly important things takes decisive action and discipline.

Effective Planning

Planning is all about establishing priorities and working within time limits to accomplish them. What promotes self-care for the minister is thinking out the way ministry will be done in the time

7 – Time Management

limits available. By identifying the items essential to the church's mission, then all other things are more non-essential and can be eliminated or delegated to others.

When there are more activities and needs to attend to than there is time, it is a matter of setting priorities and developing ways to cope that will result in a healthier and less stressed lifestyle. It is the pastor who ultimately has control over his time. One cannot blame others for an over-active schedule. Taking control of one's time is in the power of the leader. To make time to schedule one's priorities, and then to follow through on them, gives a clear message to followers and leaders alike that we are purposefully seeking direction and taking steps to fulfill godly objectives.

Scheduled calendar planning with a team or staff can effectively give direction to the organization. Strategic planning looks to the long-range future of the church and establishes goals and objectives, as well as values, to effectively evaluate any and all activities, outreaches, and ministry efforts. These types of planning sessions for mission and vision activities can also help manage people, energy, and resources needed to fulfill spiritual and practical objectives. Good planning eliminates blind attempts to accomplish the purposes of ministry.

There are many techniques and time management tools available to help ministers plan out their preaching, seasonal church calendar, and other specific issues. The old adage 'plan your work and work your plan' still has merit for those in leadership today.

Delegate Activities and Tasks to Others

When we look at Acts 6 and the selection of deacons to minister to legitimate felt needs, thus allowing the apostles to give their limited time to prayer and the preaching of the Word, we see how both time and talents were re-allocated with great results. This resulted in benefits for the whole community. The reader is encouraged to refer to the section on delegation in Chapter 10.

The lasting results we all look for are found when we determine our gifts and strengths and then concentrate on them, leaving other items of business and ministry to others who have the heart and ability to undertake those jobs. When the pastor

Finishing Well

concentrates on his strengths, he is adding depth to his ministry. When one tries to improve those areas where there is less interest or competency, then the return for the amount of effort is normally less. Concentrating on one's gifts enables the Lord to build on that which already exists, be it natural talent or spiritual giftings.

The goal of scripture is that ministers, and the leadership team, are to train and equip others for the work of the ministry. Ministers are not to do the entire ministry in a local church. They are to teach and train others for the tasks of caring for the body. In the Ephesians passage that talks about the five-fold ministry (Eph. 4:11), it goes on to discuss their function in verse 12: "to prepare God's people for works of service, so that the body of Christ may be built up until we all reach unity in the faith and in the knowledge of the Son of God and become mature, attaining to the whole measure of the fullness of Christ". When we return to this admonition of scripture, then time will be better spent training others to do the work of ministry, rather than having the minister trying to do it all.

When the church is in a position to retain a secretary or other staff, this too will help in releasing the pastor's time constraints. Even volunteer help at this level can greatly improve the effectiveness of a pastor's time management. Ministry is to be a team effort, and not a solo excursion, as is exemplified

Working with a Job Description

When it comes to how one manages time, it is valuable to look at the job description which includes the expectations and requirements within the pastorate. An adequate job description helps both the congregation and minister by defining what items of business and ministry responsibilities are in the pastor's workweek. Without such a description and working document, the minister works from a hip-pocket mentality, putting out fires, and dealing with whatever comes across their desk, often wasting time on lesser things. Dealing with the urgent, and not the important, can drain a person of vital and limited energy and passion. There are crises that must be given time and energy, but many ministry items can be planned and given appropriate attention. Stewardship of time is as important as that of finances and relationships.

7 – Time Management

The priorities of one's ministry should receive the time needed to accomplish those tasks. More ministers fail to achieve goals because they did not plan and act accordingly and missed the opportunity to give themselves fully to a particular strength, gift, or passion. People under the shepherd's care need many things, and one of them is the assurance that things will work out as God works in their lives and in the lives of their leaders. Leaders who know who they are, have a strong sense of call, and a clear understanding of their gifts, strengths, and weaknesses will be more productive as they obey the Lord in the daily outworking of ministry.

Practical Observations

We learn much from our mistakes if we are wise and observant. Understanding how we manage our time, and what works best, can also be enhanced by a little discipline in several areas that will bring a more focused and healthy ministry.

Pace Yourself

In a chapter entitled "Pace of Life', Kirk Jones (2001) writes that Jesus "moved at what I refer to as a sacred pace, a living speed characterized by peace, patience, and attentiveness" (p 50). The pace of our life seems to be getting more hectic and hurried. "Hurry" has a checklist mentality, believing that achievement and the completion of tasks create self-worth and value. Not at peace, we scurry from one appointment and ministry opportunity to the next. Driven. Pushed. Often frantic, we need to slow down, be still, and develop a pace in keeping with healthy living. Jesus Christ knew "His time had not yet come" (John 2:4) and therefore had a sense of destiny that could not be rushed.

Overload happens when we are caught up in the frantic pace of seemingly necessary activities and can't say no. Learning to evaluate what is truly important can bring the minister's time usage back into balance. We typically run out of steam before we run out of things to do, and always seem to be rushed.

Finishing Well

Know Your Limits

Knowing our limits, and then being courageous enough to say "no", can win us some extra time to recover and take care of ourselves. One of the trials ministers face is the issue of an unexpected crisis. Having built in time to sensitively respond at such times gives the Lord a chance to work with the minister, who is rested, and ready. We need to know our own limits and say no to those activities that breach them. We cannot meet all the needs of people all the time. As we realize we do not need to do everything, we will find a satisfaction and rest in ministry, having focused our time and talents where they are most needed.

Get Adequate Rest

A minister needs to develop an understanding of the ministry cycles of work and the seasons of rest and renewal. The Lord would have us flow in the Spirit, at a tempo and pace that is healthy and attractive to others. H.B. London (London, 2003) states that most ministers work long hours because they are passionate about their work and calling and are committed to serving others, not because of demands on their time. Even Jesus found time to get away from the crowds, and He encouraged His disciples to do the same. "Come away with Me by yourselves to a quiet place." (Mark 6:31) This is a call to rest in Christ. It is a call to leaders and lay people to rely on the Lord and not their own abilities or understanding.

"Sabbath time actually energizes us for more creative involvement in every area of life" (Jones, 2001, p. 44). Before we can give of ourselves to others, we need to frequently receive from the Lord His grace and love, His peace and power, His joy and rest. We need periods of rest, Sabbaths of rest, to refuel and be refreshed so we are better able to respond to needs when they come. The "Sabbath was made for man, not man for the Sabbath" (Mark 2:27).

"Attention to self-care may be perceived as a weakness, an impediment to achieving 'big-church' success" (Jones, 2001, p. 18). Yet we know that the Lord took time out and found time alone with His Father. We should do no less than follow His example. With adequate self-care and time management, leaders can stay strong and

7 – Time Management

healthy even with a busy schedule. More can be accomplished with energy to spare when we plan things out.

Summary

The Church has become a hub of activity, both spiritual and relational, and ministers who manage their time will see the blessing of the Lord in their own lives as rested people, and in the resulting relationships with others. Effectively processing life issues, evaluating how time is used, and delegating and designating ministry opportunities and needs, will result in less stress. Establishing limits on one's involvement of their personal and public time will maximize the gifts of an individual. Ministers need to practice the Mary position of honoring Christ, and not just being busy like Martha, who used her time in activities that would meet the needs of others, but failed to adequately wait on the Lord. Finishing well in ministry requires a wise use of time so that we may operate and minister with great joy.

Reviewing one's time usage, and ascertaining if time given to various activities is productive and useful, can help the minister re-adjust how they spend their time and energy. Because most ministers are dealing with a variety of topics, issues, and crises that affect their congregations, a daily time audit can help identify time wasters - busywork rather than business - and thus allow a mid-day correction. One needs to make frequent evaluations in the fast-paced, and at times on-call, lifestyle of ministry. This kind of discipline takes practice.

God created both time and space, and He desires that we accomplish His goals and plans within a workable time frame. The minister who finds balance in this area of life will find less stress and overload, as he manages within the same limited time continuum as his parishioners. One must work smarter and not harder, enjoying the small and sometimes large interruptions that come into the daily life of a shepherd of Christ. We should remind ourselves that we are to have a life that expresses the calmness, gentleness, and grace of our Lord, and not one of hurry, chaos, and shortness of breath. We are to live deeply and purposefully. In the book of Ecclesiastes (3:11), it is stated that " God will make all things beautiful in His time." Truly the

Finishing Well

Lord is working to bring all His people to a place of maturity, rest, and fulfillment. May we surrender our time into the hands of Almighty God and say like the Psalmist, "My times are in Your hands"(Psa. 31:15). Let us "trust in the Lord at all times" (62:8).

7 – Time Management

Discussion and Action Steps dealing with

TIME MANAGEMENT

Investigative Questions to Consider

1. When was the last time you took a Sabbath rest?
2. Do you post office hours and keep them?
3. Do you work more than 50 hours a week? More than 60?
4. Does your spouse, family, or friends comment frequently on your work ethic?
5. Do you miss appointments because you fail to keep them on a calendar?
6. Did you take an extended family vacation this year? Did you use all your vacation time?
7. How do you feel about the rush and busyness of our culture?
8. Does it seem you never have time for yourself?
9. What amount of time do you give to your personal devotional life? Daily? Weekly?
10. Have you considered asking for a sabbatical? What obstacles prevent taking one?
11. If you had extra time, what would you do with it? Take up a new hobby? Sign up for educational courses? Spend it with your family?
12. Has the church board given you a job description of expectations and responsibilities?

Finishing Well

Action Steps

1. Keep a time log of activities for two weeks. Review with your board and family.

2. Plan a family vacation and follow up on it.

3. Schedule a monthly planning day, where you get away for the sole purpose of seeking God for ministry direction and setting of priorities.

4. Consider hiring a church secretary if your church does not currently have one.

5. Do an assessment of members' skills to assist you in delegating some tasks to free up more time for essential duties.

6. Take a Time Management Seminar to improve your use of time.

CHAPTER 8

ACCOUNTABILITY

The Bible gives us a great example of what ministers need to do in Psalms 78:72. "And David shepherded them with integrity of heart; with skillful hands he led them."

Accountable relationships for the leader deal with one's personal integrity. To finish well in a ministry career is a teamwork effort with others, such as a godly spouse, a support board of elders, and peers who are genuine, all contributing to keeping a leader on track. Clinton (1988) sees leadership development in the accountable experiences that test or check one's integrity. These may be value checks, temptation checks, tests over conflicts against a minister's vision, persecution, loyalty and restitution issues, among other things, that God allows to develop a mature leader. They are issues that call into question one's values and deep beliefs, and in the end make the minister accountable (p. 60). Fifty-five percent of pastors in one study indicated that they had a small group to which they were accountable. (The Parsonage, 2001)

The Bible is full of passages and narratives that deal with the issue of personal accountability and the consequences of sin. Integrity of one's life is so valued, that when Paul wrote to Timothy and Titus about the requirements for leadership, he included the issues of integrity, lifestyle, and maturity (1 Tim. 3:1-13; Tit. 1:5-9). Luke records the words of Jesus in 12:48, "From everyone who has been given much, much will be demanded; and from the one who has been entrusted with much, much more will be asked." The context of this passage is that of stewardship and responsibility to the tasks one has been given. In the light of the coming of Christ, servants and workers are to remain faithful to the work they have been given. There will be a day of accounting.

Finishing Well

Develop a Support Team

When Moses was faced with the warring tribe of Amalek, he was supported by two men, Aaron and Hur, as he held the staff of God above his head. This team effort resulted in victory for Moses and the people of God. Battles are won when we work in the power of the Spirit and in cooperation with others. The Christian life and ministry was not meant to be a solo journey, but one in which all are working together in their various areas of ability. Support is one issue that surfaces in the evaluation of ministers and longevity in ministry. With support of a spouse, friends, and associates, ministers are more likely to succeed and be sustained over the long haul. Those without accountability groups or a network of caring individuals fail more often to achieve fruitful ministry.

Accountability As a Safeguard

Studies by Hands and Fehr (1993) indicated that clergy who transgressed sexual boundaries were generally "impoverished as far as intimacy with self, others, and God (were) concerned" (p. 43). Those who were isolated and unaccountable to others had more opportunities to fail in this area. "Only 4% of ministers involved in moral indiscretions were ever found out" (Exley, *Perils of Power*, 1995, p. 75). This statement means there is estimated to be many more who have failed morally, and that they have not been a part of an accountable group that knew their indiscretions. Human sexuality must be understood by all individuals as a gift of God and not a burden to bear. Those in the role of clergy are no less human, and have the same struggles and challenges of purity and sexual chastity as do the people of the faith community.

Our need for intimacy with ourselves, with God, and with others is enhanced when we accept our sexuality, and maintain a biblical standard of holiness in regards to our use of sexual intimacy within marriage only. Hands & Fehr (1993) pose the thought that once self-esteem, the absence of shame, and then intimacy, or emotional closeness, have been met and developed, then sexual integration and gratification can occur in its rightful role. Often those clergy who have experienced the painful results of inappropriate

8 – Accountability

sexual conduct find out that they are lacking in the other areas of self-esteem and emotional well-being. Intimacy is more than a sexual act; it is a composite of our personality, our need for emotional support, and spiritual acceptance. Biblical counseling and an inward look can reveal not only the problems, but the answers, that are found in the Word of God through redemptive care in the context of supporting our clergy.

The Bible has much to say about the need for purity and holiness in the life of believers and leaders. Scripture indicates that there is a great responsibility to sexual purity, thought life, and actions. A failure in this area can create grounds for dismissal from ministry itself. The need for self-discipline and responsibility is critical.

Reporting Is Accountability

General accountable reporting should be to one's job description and to one's leadership team of elders, and should be done on a regular basis. Reviews of how one is doing in ministry, perhaps on a quarterly or yearly basis, are a useful tool for accountability.

There is a moral and morale problem among clergy today. Both need our attention as to the roots of what is happening, or might happen, in the life of a minister. Developing a support system for clergy is one of several tools that can bolster faith, encourage a reality check, and affirm each other. Galatians 5:24 says we are to crucify fleshly passions and desires. One author (Exley, *Perils of Power*, p. 37) reminds us that there are four things to do to maintain victory: maintain intimacy with God and your spouse; set appropriate boundaries; remain accountable; and expose temptations as soon as you sense their presence.

As pastors are a busy group, it is not easy to schedule time, and even if time can be found, it may be uncomfortable to meet with other peers for the purpose of strengthening each other in the work of the Lord, and maintaining a personal walk with God. One must be intentional in developing lasting relationships of trust and openness. Oswald makes the comment that "leaderless groups don't work" (Oswald, 1991, p. 98). When small groups meet without someone taking the lead, the dynamics become such that little is accomplished, and the groups flounder and often cease to exist. A facilitator in a group of clergy from different denominational backgrounds can keep the group on track and dealing with the issues and concerns at hand. It is suggested they be paid to facilitate self-care clergy groups. It is also noted that clergy groups from the same denomination fail as well, due to self-interests and more competitive relationships within that same denomination. Superiors or denominational executives have too many close ties to the career and referral of ministers to make them effective and safe facilitators. A care group needs to be a safe place where sensitive information is shared without the fear of it getting to leadership positions. A facilitator needs to have three qualities: competence, sensitivity, and confidentiality (Oswald, 1991, p. 39).

Depending on Other People

Bruce Reed of the Grubb Institute in London developed a theory now called the Grubb Oscillation Theory. Grubb stated that individuals oscillate between two states: one of depending on self, and the other of depending on other people. Oswald uses the term "extradependence" as "a state in which I am dependent upon a source outside of me ('extra') that is caring and trustworthy and allows me to let go; be de-roled; play; and move into Sabbath Time and an experience of grace" (Oswald, 1991, p. 43). Opposite to *extradependence* is *intradependence,* where individuals are self-sufficient, self-contained, and the main source of strength is that person alone.

A small accountability group with an appropriate facilitator and guidelines can assist ministers to be renewed and healed by not being in the primary role of leader or director, but in that of a receiver, just like their parishioners on Sunday morning. Groups of individuals can be a safeguard for the minister, to guard his character, so he doesn't destroy the gift. Jeff Lucas, a minister from Great Britain, adds a similar comment, that "what our gifts have built, our character has the potential to destroy" (Lucas, 2004). Being an equal with others, and not the leader, is valuable in that one has the opportunity to be open, honest, and more genuine in their responses to a peer group. Family, friendships, peer groups, the congregational setting - all can be valid resources for growth and awareness of a person's spiritual state.

8 – Accountability

It is this author's experience that while serving in a closed country overseas, the main support group consisted of ministers from the same organization. The availability of others from different groups was present, but in a closed country that was suspicious of all Christian activity, we kept very casual relationships so as not to jeopardize each other's work. We needed a support group and a facilitator. There were too many instances of vulnerability that caused tension and stressed relationships.

Maintenance of Healthy Habits of Accountability

To be accountable to someone is to be aware that we must answer for our actions as a responsible part of living. Ministers can find themselves in a place where they are operating from a lone ranger position, with no accountable relationships to challenge or give guidance and feedback for their message or their ministry. It is healthiest if every person submits to others for feedback and input. God brought us into this world by way of the family unit for the health and welfare of each newborn. There is a parallel in the spiritual outworking of our lives. We are born again into the kingdom of God and then given a family - the church - with its relationships of wiser, older, and more mature loving individuals who teach, train, and instruct us in the way of Christian living.

The dangers of not having accountable relationships is that our ideas, views, and even dreams are not tested by reality, or in a social setting, to be clarified, and even challenged. Scripture says, "In the multitude of counselors, there is safety." A minister needs to "accept the responsibility for exercising spiritual discipline which will enable him to overcome the habits of a lifetime" (Exley, *Perils of Power*, 1995, p. 18). When we share our thoughts with other responsible people, we are then open to critical thinking and perhaps a re-evaluation of our ideas or planned activities. God does work through people to give us guidance and to increase our knowledge by sharing thoughts and spiritual insight from a variety of sources. As genuine Christ-like character grows over time and in relationships, an accountable plan for one's actions and the inner workings of the Spirit can be a valuable tool which the Lord can use. "Ministry flows out of being" (Clinton, 1988, p. 46), and this reveals the relationship

Finishing Well

between who we are and how we manage and do ministry. Accountable relationships take time and energy, and like any other relationship, will have their moments when the process of intimacy at a level of accountable openness is slow, and at times, cumbersome. In the end, when we have opened our hearts to another trusted person, we have an opportunity to be genuinely real and vulnerable. Vulnerability is not an area where ministers like to go, as they are perceived, and at times self-deceived, to believe that they are almost perfect, or at least have a special knowledge or edge on any given situation. Reality shows us all that we are in need of a Christ-like humbleness to submit to the Father's will and way. Proverbs shows us the benefits of seeking wisdom from God, as it alone will "guard the course of the just and protect the way of His faithful ones" (Proverbs 2:8).

An accountable relationship asks the questions related to personal or professional purpose, intent, and attitude, and are a means of follow-up on projects - be they personal goals or ministry goals. Purpose questions can be addressed in accountable settings: What is your intent or purpose? What is the attitude of the minister? What is the motive for doing certain tasks? Are the tasks a priority to the mission of the church or individual?

A mentoring relationship is not primarily for accountability, but that value may be helpful at certain points in the relationship. Most accountable relationships have to do with giving guidance and helping one to do what they said they would do. Accountability keeps the individual in a position in which they must answer for their words and actions. This is healthy, and can enhance and encourage, as well as give guidance in the performance of duties, or the evaluation of activities within an organization.

Establishing a Ministry Philosophy

Over a lifetime of ministry, a leader develops some basic principles of leadership and core values. The processing of one's life experiences is the maturing process that brings leaders into a better and more effective place of ministry. Clinton suggests that the development of a ministry philosophy will assist the leader in knowing what he believes and the principles on which he manages his

8 – Accountability

life and ministry. When such a document is created and modified over time, the leader can then be accountable to his own ministry philosophy. This would be a document that is crafted around basic value statements, core beliefs, and principles one believes in and operates by in everyday life. Such a statement, or written document, clarifies the truths by which one manages life and any future issues. It is a "standard of excellence for oneself".

This author has found that in writing out his own ministry philosophy, there came clarity of purpose, and a basis or foundation for how he managed in the past and would continue in the future. The Lord gave strength and insight as this book was created. It has served as a reminder of the lessons learned in the crises of life, as well as the good things that God brought as a result of faithful service to the call. A philosophy of ministry also acts as a reminder of what one has purposed in their heart to do, given the opportunity, and leadership of the Holy Spirit. One can go back to that document to test and challenge any new opportunities or proposed ideas and values.

"Leaders with a good ministry philosophy usually finish well" (Clinton, 1988, p. 201). They finish well because they have challenged themselves to remain faithful to their ministry philosophy and objectives. They finish well because they bring self-discipline to their lives that is often lacking in others. They know their own weaknesses and propensity to be lazy or haphazard about staying true to Christ or their purpose in life, and thus submit themselves to the authority of Christ and to accountable relationships to maintain their higher goals and expectations.

During the life of a leader, there are a variety of ministry development issues that create one of four possible responses. Clinton (1999, p. 201) lists these patterns as:

1. Those who drop out of ministry, which are many.
2. Those who have plateaued, which is the majority of leaders.
3. Those who are disciplined, which represent a few.
4. Those who continue to grow and finish well, which represent some leaders.

Finishing Well

Clinton senses that those who do not finish well in life and ministry have not responded well to the experiences of ministry, or who have strayed from their ministry philosophy, if indeed they had one at all. Leaders benefit from placing themselves in accountable relationships in which they can profit from other peoples' experiences and knowledge.

Again, a system of accountability should include peers, staff, or friends. These people, plus a personal ministry philosophy and a self-disciplined life, will bring added strength and the challenge to maintain one's integrity, focus, and direction to accomplish the purposes of God for their life and ministry. Ministers, like all leaders, need people in their lives who not only follow them, but have the freedom to speak into their lives, to challenge attitudes and motives, and to support them by encouragement and prayer.

8 – Accountability

Discussion and Action Steps dealing with

ACCOUNTABILITY

1. Within your church, do you have a policy manual that establishes safeguards for financial transactions?

2. Do you have a written document or forms for the handling of any funds or reimbursements for ministry expenses?

3. Have you established boundaries for your counseling or contact time with parishioners?

4. Do you have regular meetings or contact with an accountability partner for your personal growth and spiritual life?

5. Do you have a list of questions or guidelines for that accountable relationship?

6. To whom do you give account for the hours of ministry time?

7. Have you secured your Internet access from invasive and inappropriate web sites?

8. Do you allow a designated IT person to access your computer, both at home and the office, to review your website activities?

9. Have you been faithful in keeping your spouse or board informed of your use of time, church vehicle, church credit cards, etc.?

10. If you struggle with temptations or addictions, to whom do you go for help?

11. Are you okay with having leadership over you in accountable relationships?

Finishing Well

12. Does your ministry and ministry team align with the biblical requirements for leadership?

Action Steps

1. Set up a computer filtering system that requires you to post or notify accountable persons of your Internet activities.

2. Invite a qualified IT person to monitor your computer Internet on a regular basis, and give authorization for them to report to your spouse and church board.

3. Write out a policy and procedures document for any transactions involving finances, counseling, or other pastoral duties to safeguard both the church and its leadership.

4. Do a risk assessment for all church programs and ministries.

5. Develop protocol for selecting board members, staff, and church volunteers.

CHAPTER 9

NURTURING RELATIONSHIPS

Ministry is all about relationships. Maintaining healthy relationships with our Lord, with our spouse and family, and then with the church and the people in our sphere of influence requires that we understand the stressors that come in living out our lives.

A Definition of Relational Stress

What is Relational Stress?

There are many definitions of stress, some more medical than spiritual, but we find that one by Pappas (1995) clarifies a new way to look at stress:

> Stress is an invitation to coordinate with God's agenda. If you are a goal-oriented person, interruptions are more than interruptions in schedule, agenda, or energy; they are irritations, frustrations, and time and energy wasters. In the face of our definition of self, ministry, and agenda, God is offering us the divine agenda and it comes to us in the guise of stress. Stress is present to teach us that the interruptions in our agenda are our spiritual ministry agenda" (p.139).

Stress causes each of us to reconsider what we are doing, and who we are becoming. Stress should be seen as an indicator that we need to have the touch of God to not only help us in our stress, but also to teach us His ways in the midst of ministry and life. Pappas (1995) examined the "crossed energy - the emotional energy that is the result of a pastor's expectations crossing with his or her experience" (p. 139). Pappas claims, and rightly so, that when "crossed energy can be aligned, when one's understanding and expectations become consonant with the realities out there, then stress can be transformed into a strength, breakdowns into breakthroughs, and energy is released for growth and ministry" (p. 139).

Stowell (1997) says that the ultimate test of shepherding is when we, like Christ, are willing to commit ourselves even to our enemies' needs. Holding steady in the midst of accusations and misunderstandings, and taking the high road of grace and love, allows the Holy Spirit to bring the issue to pass in a more constructive way than one might normally have handled it. Even Jesus washed the feet of His betrayer. We too, must be willing to the wash the feet of those who may, in the end, cause us harm. Learning to trust the Lord in any given situation for His grace, love, and insight comes with experience from real life situations. Staying humble as a servant of the Lord (Phil. 2:6-8; 1 Peter 5:6-7) allows our example to speak to the other person's life. Sometimes words are not necessary as much as a gracious and loving spirit.

Personal Stress

There is a wide variety of personality types that enter the ministry. God has shown us that He can choose and use anyone, no matter if they are introverts or extroverts, or any number of other variables. Stress occurs when we are overloaded, overextended, or working outside of our gifts and strengths. It can also be due to the expectations of oneself or of others. We discuss this more thoroughly in Chapter 10 - the conflicts that arise due to demands and expectations.

Congregational Stress

Each local congregation has its own living and dynamic cultural identity and ways of operating that the minister must understand and work with or stressors will eventually increase. Pappas (1995) writes, "The basic source of stress in communication and authority patterns occurs when the pastor has one form in mind and the congregation is used to operating in another" (p. 79). With a variety of expectations and assumptions, stress results. To identify the different patterns of communication, and then to discuss the need to change these patterns with your leadership team, will assist in

9 – *Nurturing Relationships*

reducing undue friction. Pastoral stress occurs when there is a deliberate attempt to change existing patterns or even to maintain the status quo, which involves more emotional energy (p. 80). "Trust grows out of relationships, and the very heart of relationships is communication" (Exley, *Perils of Power*, 1995, p. 92).

Pappas (1995) and McIntosh (1999) both argue that size dynamics of a church is another ministry stressor that needs to be considered when looking for answers for our ministers. When pastoral expectation for growth to the next level of ministry - be it size, income, or another measurable indicator - is not met, then stress is the result. When a church is small or average size, there is often stress on the pastor to bring the church to a more "successful" level of ministry. Often however, both the congregation and pastoral giftings are unsuited to such a dynamic change. Faithfulness to the task of ministry life in such a setting is the most important role the leader can bring to the church.

Too often, our comparisons with larger and more dynamic churches bring jealously, resentment, and a non-Christian attitude of competition or arrogance. Pappas (1995) again says that not only is there stress from the congregational or pastoral expectations for growth, but should growth occur, "the original membership often feels alienation, not victory and joy... The pastor who expects elation from these members, only to get alienation, will experience stress" (p. 87). To combat the tension that exists today for those in leadership, there is a very real need on the part of the pastor to evaluate his gifts and style as they relate to the overall ministry. If there is a mismatch, then it may be time to move on to another ministry context where there is a better fit. Another possibility for alleviating stress is to try and change the size level of the congregation to match the skill level of the pastor. Although this is often the direction many churches are going, there is the added stress for the congregation and pastor of often unwelcome changes.

Congregational Culture

When dealing with the complex issues of leadership in a congregation, there is also the area of the local congregational culture, which includes the lifestyles, backgrounds, and sociological issues that are dominant in a particular setting. There are many books out on the subject of contextualization of the gospel for today's society, whereby we develop a variety of gospel presentations to suit or fit the local worldview of the audience. This does not mean we water down the gospel, but that we present ministry is such a way that it clearly speaks to the issues of the felt needs of the general population. The reality is that our society is changing quickly and the status quo of the life of the church must be modified or reshaped if it is to connect the good news of Jesus Christ to spiritually cynical, and often closed-minded hearers. When we begin to see that God wants us to trust Him as we make changes in the way we do ministry, but not in the message, then we will see His provision by the Spirit of God for accomplishing those tasks, and touching lives for Him. Our dependency is on Him alone, not ourselves, our programs, or our charisma. The church has always been called to be a light on a hill, an outpost of hope for those in need of a spiritual relationship with Christ.

A Personal Walk With God

The self-discipline and daily spiritual habits of a minister, if strong and maintained, give strength and grace to the outward ministry efforts. Exercising one's will to intentionally stay strong in the inner life is vital to the health of the church. Paul the Apostle wrote in Colossian 1:24-29 that God made him a minister to fulfill the will of God. This would require a constant vigilance against temptations, old ways, and the works of the flesh. "Life reveals the condition of the heart" (Brandt and Blackaby, 1997, p. 117).

Spouse and Family

Ministerial marriages are under the added pressure of life in the fast lane, with all of its activities, programs, and emergencies. Unless the marriage relationship is protected from these disruptions and given adequate attention, clergy marriages will suffer the consequences. Marriages and families do have their own stress-producing issues, but it appears more likely that the family is affected

9 – *Nurturing Relationships*

by the added stress of a busy ministerial lifestyle. The stress that occurs in a ministry life of relationships, crises, conflicts, and general church organization and expectations may have an adverse effect on the pastor's family. Establishing boundaries and priorities that safeguard the family would include time out and away from ministry, short dates and outings, and time with the children.

What are some ways that have worked to maintain balance in the ministry so that marriages are strong, stable, and safe? Defining ministry roles for husband and wife sets boundaries to what is acceptable involvement and can limit over-commitment. Marriages need to develop common goals but identify different roles. Pastoral life is not "two-for-one", in that the wife may have focuses other than the church.

The clergyman may be everyone's pastor, but perhaps fail at pastoring his own wife and family. One must initiate productive conversations and activities to enhance the home relationships. It is too easy to bring one's work home and thereby miss the growth issues on the home front. It is very easy to get so engaged in other peoples' lives with all their issues, that there develops a gap between the pastor and his spouse and children, with little or nothing in common except ministry. Develop hobbies or interests that are totally separate from ministry life. Too many have "gained the whole world", but lost their family in the process.

Speaking Up for Your Family

Ministers need to be very forthright with their boards and congregations as to what they need to maintain balance in the ministry so that their own marriages are strong, stable, and safe. What good is it if we win our world and lose our family?

Ministers often comment that they are overworked and underpaid, which contributes to discouragement in the home. These need to be addressed by the pastor to his board on a regular basis.

Most people are very understanding of the need for privacy for the pastor and their family. Establishing office hours will assist the majority of callers and those needing help. By adjusting one's work schedule, there will be other times that are less hectic or demanding. Again, delegation and a firm resolve to protect the family from

Finishing Well

intrusions will go a long way in alleviating stress. There are a host of seminars, retreat centers, and counselors willing to assist clergy families with great love and understanding. The Appendix lists several resources available for ministers and their families.

Wives of Ministers

Dr. Archibald Hart (Hart, 2004), speaking at a luncheon for pastors and their spouses, said that wives of clergy need to do four things to finish well:

1. Find their own support group
2. Identify and embrace their own purpose and ministry.
3. Grow by maintaining balance and health.
4. Care for themselves. (No pseudo-sacrifices)

Of all the primary relationships a minister has, it is their spouse that is their lifelong companion. A healthy marriage relationship will do much to safeguard against temptations and addictions, and ensure the emotional strength needed for the journey called ministry. As spouses serve alongside the minister, it is a place of vulnerability to the inquiring eyes of those being served. By making intentional efforts to keep a healthy balance between public and private life, ministry homes can be happy, fruitful, and places of refuge.

Interpersonal Relationships

It is the interpersonal relationships that test our character and commitment to be a shepherd-minister in a local church setting. When conflicts arise between parishioners and the leader that is a test of the leader's heart and values. This is the area which had the highest stress for ministers in most of the surveys evaluated.

The challenge is to be the same person - fair, honest, a man of integrity - in both one's public and private life. This kind of consistency and stability reveals an integrity of heart, where there is no duplicity or hypocrisy. Many pastors have had little if any training in seminary in developing interpersonal skills.

9 – Nurturing Relationships

The multitude of interpersonal relationships brings a richness and depth of love and life to the pastoral calling that is not found in most other professions. The sheer variety of in-depth relationships that develop over time creates a deep love, respect, and a sense of holy privilege to the minister. Who else knows the depths and heights, the inner conflicts and the hopes of people that only a caretaker of souls – the pastor - can experience? This trusted relationship with people in all walks of life and in all phases of spiritual and emotional health can be both exhilarating and humbling, as well as a burden, as we see God working or trying to work though us to bring people to Christ.

This overexposure to some people and their problems can often jeopardize the relationship, as some people may indeed blame the pastor for the way God is working in their lives. As a representative of the Lord, pastors are a prime target for venting frustrations and hurt that congregants may have in other areas of their lives.

It is a wise pastor who recognizes that they are in a role, not as the answer man, but as a person who empathizes and at times sympathizes with their congregant's issues. To stay effective in ministry for the long term, ministers need to develop a thick skin but maintain a sensitive and caring heart. Conflict and unjust criticism will come to every person, and especially those who claim to be representatives of God. When one recognizes that they are a part of a long line of ministers sent from God, like the prophets of old, then they will gain strength of character and stay the course in the midst of troubled people, who need and desire help from the Lord. Ministers are not alone in their interpersonal relationships and all that comes with them. They are a part of a select group of people whom the Lord has called and equipped to share the love and grace of the Savior. The task of undershepherds is to represent Christ by both word and deed, by modeling Christian values and gracious love of Christ to a people without a shepherd.

There is inter-connectedness in all these areas of ministry life. Lasting and mature healthy relationships occur when leadership is consistent in their Christian values with the resulting actions. Trust is earned, not just given. It is the small everyday decisions and courtesies that endear ministers to their people. People want to know that a pastor can be trusted with confidences shared in a counseling session, and that their struggles, hopes, and dreams are honored by this one called "pastor".

The Loneliness Factor

Boers (1991, p. 131) cites Henri Nouwen from *'In Reaching Out'* that:

> Loneliness is one of the most universal sources of human suffering today. Psychiatrists and clinical psychologists speak about it as the most frequently expressed complaint and the root not only of an increasing number of suicides but also of alcoholism, drug abuse, (and) different psychosomatic symptoms. Boers says, "My loneliness isn't necessarily caused by my call, although it might be exacerbated by it" (p. 131).

The reasons for loneliness in ministry stem from a number of related issues. Boers says that working alone, playing the role of pastor, isolation from the extended family, and pastoring the flock with no time for outsiders, all contribute to the sense of loneliness.

There are some rewards of ministerial loneliness that we should consider before we say that loneliness is all bad. There is the potential for spiritual growth in solitude, be it prayer, reflection, or good thinking. Pastors should be more appreciative of healthy relationships and contacts when they do occur.

The way out of loneliness for ministers involves seeking out friendships with other pastors; frank awareness of their own needs; developing stronger home relationships; and establishing friendships within the church.

Summary

Ministry is all about relationships at a variety of levels of involvement. The pastorate brings with it a wide range of human responses to life. Understanding people, and having the wisdom and grace to minister to the needs of people, is in large part where

9 – *Nurturing Relationships*

ministry occurs. It is in the everyday dealings with people and their circumstances and issues that the minister is given the opportunity to speak for Christ, to bring comfort, direction, correction, or encouragement. Ministers are in a fabulous calling, where the Lord gives them access to be agents of change and hope; where they are allowed into the hidden life of their parishioners. From time to time, there is a great working of the Spirit to assist in transforming lives that are broken to the healing power of Christ. At other times, it is the listening ear or caring touch that brings hope to a seemingly hopeless situation.

Most ministers learn pastoral care from experience or having worked with someone who modeled compassionate and strong pastoral care practices. Very few seminaries and training centers have classes on the subject of compassion or how to work with people. There should be more emphasis in our training of ministers to include the interpersonal aspects of ministry, with large doses of ethics, sociology, human dynamics, and psychological insights into humanity.

The variety of personalities represented in a congregation need a caring pastor to love them and to bring them to Christ. Even as there are strong and weak personalities - the extrovert and introvert - there is the antagonist and critical person who needs the love of Christ and the love of their pastor. Oswald (1988) looks at personality type and leadership style. The insight gained from studying this topic helps one to manage and minister more effectively to those within the church and community.

Surveys indicate that many ministers are overworked and underpaid which contributes to discouragement in the home. These issues need to be addressed by the pastor with his board on a regular basis.

The minister has the keys to safeguard his personal relationship with Christ, his spouse and family, and the ongoing relationships that are a part of pastoral care. Effective and healthy ministers make the added effort to ensure that things are well on the home front, as well as the responsibility to the larger congregation and community.

Finishing Well

Discussion and Action Steps dealing with

NURTURING RELATIONSHIPS

Investigative Questions to Consider

1. When it comes to Sabbath rest, do you take regular days off?

2. Do you work as hard on family relationships as you do with church members?

3. Have you kept a 'date night' with your spouse; children?

4. Can you say 'no' to appointments and opportunities in order to safeguard promises made to family, self, or friends?

5. Does it seem like ministry never ends?

6. Have your spouse or children vocalized their disappointment in your inability to maintain balance between ministry and family?

7. Are you intentional in seeking out friends, and availing yourself of opportunities to meet new people for personal relationships, and not just church-related ministry?

8. During family time, are you easily interrupted by church business?

9. How have your children responded/reacted to your calling as a minister?

10. Do you have children who are in rebellion primarily because of your ministry calling?

11. If your marriage were struggling with an issue, would you seek out counsel, or try to solve it yourself?

9 – Nurturing Relationships

12. How healthy is your family and spousal relationships?

Action Steps

1. Establish and maintain family devotions and fun times.

2. Develop creative ways to involve your family in ministry.

3. Set up boundaries to safeguard your family from intrusions from church demands.

4. Involve your spouse and family in planning a family vacation or outings.

5. Find new ways of expressing your love to your family.

6. Safeguard planned family time from interruptions.

Chapter 10

Demands and Expectations

Pastoral care is a never-ending cycle of meeting needs, training leaders, and discipling the people under one's leadership. Sixty-eight percent of pastors in one study (Rowell, 1998) said that they expected too much from themselves. Only 7% responded that they felt pressure from their boards, and only one-fifth felt pressure from their congregations. It appears that many expectations and demands come from within one's own lifestyle. Pastors are the predominant ones responsible for long work hours and a pressured lifestyle. Stress and burnout issues come home to roost at the pastor's own office. When there are feelings of stress, one needs to see this as a warning system that things need to change.

Defining the Pastoral Role

A great help for the servant leader is to place some guidelines in one's job description that assist the minister and congregation concerning work load. Too many congregations and ministers operate from an "always on call" mentality. True, crises must be attended to, but there can be more scheduling of other activities to release the pastor from the constant demand for their time. Again, delegation of some ministry tasks can be made to responsible people, deacons, and mature believers, so as to free up more of the minister's time for major responsibilities. Speaking openly with one's board or governing body about the pressures and demands can assist in clarifying one's role in a shepherd capacity.

There are unrealistic expectations of some congregants and ministers themselves which tend to place a drain on the minister's energy and spiritual vitality. There are limits for what any one person can do and know to serve effectively. Finding those limits may include listening to your spouse, your board, or your body. To realize that we are not the Savior for every situation and need, nor do we need to be in control at every business meeting or ministry event, can save one from a lot of frustration. Interpersonal stress over ministry

Finishing Well

expectations can be reduced if ministers will give up their ego and self-esteem issues, and trust in Christ for His approval and direction. Forty percent (Rowell, 1998, p.86) of pastors have a hard time saying 'no' to requests for their time and input. Sanford (1982, p.32) says, "Frankness and genuineness are always more healing than the best of the egocentric posturing."

Transformation of ministry happens when we are willing to humbly assess our role as pastor with the congregation in mind. To develop a job description or ministry description is one way of lessening stress in the ministry. The process, if done in conjunction with responsible lay leadership, will both enlighten the tasks of a minister to the congregation; and their expectations to the minister. Working out the functions of leadership in a local setting will be the more difficult and long-term project. Hopefully this experience will assist all parties to spend the energy and spiritual vitality in the right places. What we do, in large part, is a product of our personality and the demands or expectations placed upon us by ourselves or others. Fruitful and faithful ministry takes place when we have defined our leadership roles and act within those definitions. Transforming ministry stress into actions of love and commitment are the goals for every minister called of God. Too many times, ministers become all things to all men and are left wondering where the joy of serving the Lord went. Again, we are called to work *with* God in the redemptive and shepherding role and not *for* Him, so we must strive to know our place and role in the kingdom of God.

Pappas (1995) sees stress buildup as energy that crosses with task-oriented pastoral role definitions (p.60). He goes on to relate the different, insufficient, or inefficient ways in which ministers relate to their role as a leader. Stress buildup over time in this area is a primary killer of shepherds who are not working in the area of their gifting, or are in the wrong place of ministry. Either adjustments need to be made on the part of the pastor, or a change is most likely coming - either burnout or a forced exit.

Developing a Pace of Living

There are several things that ministers can do to help alleviate stress and the drive to perform. Ministers should take a closer look at

10 – Demands and Expectations

Jesus' style of relating to ministry needs and find that He, too, took time off from a busy schedule to get rest, to reflect, and to recuperate. Jesus, as our Shepherd, had all authority (Matt.28:18-20; Mark 10:42-45; John 5:18-24; John 7:15-17) given to him but he managed it in such a way that there was a cadence, a rhythm of life, that was rested and open to interruptions. When pastors can set a pace of living, like breathing - a natural flow of life - then the pastor is in a better mind-set, and spiritual energy and health can come forth to meet the needs of the congregation. When pastors work an average of 55 hours a week, their energy level is due to decrease. Time management here is of great value in that by setting priorities and scheduling time off, as well as allotting time for family and recreation, a balance can be restored to the pastor's life. "Without spiritual energy, religious activism is nothing more than a round of beneficent activities that quickly run out of purpose, passion, and support" (London, 2003 p.180).

Realizing that one is not invincible, and is susceptible to burnout and exhaustion, the wise minister will step aside from some opportunities that present themselves, so as to better serve in areas of their strengths and giftings. In a great book by Richard Swenson, *Margin*, the author takes a long, hard look at the drivenness of our society and thus our ministries. Swenson (1992) believes that too many feel it their duty to do all they can, and thus are driven to meet the ever-increasing demands on their time and energy. Developing a margin - that space between events and our limits - will create a rested and contented person.

Jones (2001, p. 39) makes note of three addictions that often surface in a caregiver's life: "adrenaline, achievement, and affirmation." Each of these often pushes and motivates pastors to do more than what is required of them. Getting a balance, and realizing that there is never an end to doing ministry, that there will always be uncompleted tasks and unmet needs, will help prolong the minister's life and effectiveness. Jones quotes: "Mohandas Gandhi is reported to have said, 'There is more to life than increasing its speed.'" (Jones, 2001, p. 50). The opposite of a busy person is the one who has plateaued in their ministry. These are typically those who have gained some skill and experience, and then stopped developing as a leader for Christ. No longer a lifelong learner, they run on old ways of

Finishing Well

managing, doing ministry repeats, and often go into a maintenance mode of operating (Clinton, 1988). This type of attitude can create stress for the congregation.

The expectations and demands of ministry have an impact on every leader. How one adjusts and copes with the ministry life-style will often determine the longevity of one's ministry. John Johnson, in an article entitled 'Learning How to Lead When the Honeymoon Ends', (Roberts, 1999, p. 159), quotes Joseph Sittleras: "There are a myriad of demands, each exhausting a portion of you... Their time, their vocational focus, their vision of the central task, their mental life, and their contemplative 'acreage' are 'all under the chopper'. Such fragmentation leads to a loss of bearings, a dizzying occupational oscillation, and a well that has run dry" (Ecology of Faith, p. 78). Delegation is a great tool to help in this area of overload.

Delegation as a Tool for Leadership

The Old Testament account of Moses and Jethro (Exod. 18:13-27) indicates that God gave Moses help and understanding in the midst of his overload. The responsibilities that had come to Moses were overwhelming and Jethro stated that it was not good. Delegation was advised and seventy elders were given the responsibility to manage the problems on a more local level. This helpful insight brought Moses relief from the stress of leadership and included other capable people to minister at various levels of the organization. We see here that delegation of duties to others did not diminish the accountability of Moses, but gave him the structure to better serve his people. Delegation freed the leader, who was reluctant at first, from the areas where others were just as capable to administrate as himself. Prior to the delegation of responsibilities to qualified people, Moses was one busy and stressed-out leader.

Gangel (1989) sees in Exodus 18:16-17 that God had a solution for His servant, Moses. Those chosen were given the same spirit Moses had and would in the end help carry the burden of the people, "so that you will not have to carry it alone" (Exod.18:17). This division of the work load brought about a double blessing - relieving Moses of being the primary worker, and involving other

10 – *Demands and Expectations*

people in ministry tasks. Efficiency and effectiveness resulted in a more stable and peaceful organization.

The New Testament indicates in Acts 6 that the apostles who were overworked were given help in the form of deacons who attended to matters, thus freeing up the apostles for a more focused ministry. Strong leaders recognize the need to bring others alongside into active participation in ministry if the work is to expand.

Just because one can do many things does not mean that they should. True success in life comes when we focus on our strengths and the places where our gifts and abilities are most effective. Delegation of responsibilities to others who are more gifted or inclined to fulfill those responsibilities with joy and passion will result in a team effort and greater success for the ministry as a whole. That person to whom we give authority is now the responsible party for accomplishing the assigned ministry task.

Delegation of authority and responsibility releases the leader to be more effective in areas of their strengths and passion. Enlisting qualified people, and releasing them to participate in areas of their giftedness and ability, brings about more of a team effort and less of the lone ranger style of management. Delegating to the right people, with clearly defined tasks and projected outcomes, assists the organization to move forward in its primary goals and mission. Leaders can and should delegate authority and responsibility, but are ultimately accountable for all such designations.

How does one delegate?

There are several things that need to be addressed in this area. One is that the leader defines what they expect from the delegated person's role. Defining with a job description, procedures included, plus expectations of outcomes, all assist in the process of ensuring success. Again, one needs to delegate to people who are qualified to some degree, and committed to the overall mission of the organization. One needs to take the time to answer questions such as what should be delegated, to whom, when, why, and how, so that by establishing a procedure and process of delegation, the individuals involved have a very clear definition of expectations and outcomes.

Finishing Well

Once a person has been selected and given some training and guidelines, the leader needs to reinforce their belief that they have the right person. Encouragement and words of positive affirmation will build up and strengthen the new worker. A second task is to assure that the authority is not undermined by the leader or others. Let the person determine their work habits or how they will manage the project. Otherwise, the leader is trying to micro-manage his staff or volunteers. A leader needs to ask for frequent reviews or reports from the delegated person, not as a way of control, but as a way of keeping abreast of the progress, and as a tool to assist in staying on track. Providing adequate resources, be it people or funds, all contribute to progress and a smooth flow towards desired goals.

Many in leadership have not been able to release jobs and tasks to qualified people, more from a platform of insecurity or fear that the job will not be done or done right. The element of trust comes into play here. Leaders need to learn to trust others and God for new people to whom they can give responsibilities and the authority to carry out assigned tasks. Over time, many pastors have taken back delegated authority due to their own failure to come alongside those individuals during difficult times. It is true that some tasks were perhaps given to the wrong person, but that is a learning process in itself. Knowing your people - their skills, gifts, callings, and commitment to the leader and the church - all contribute to making good choices.

More can be accomplished by leaders through delegation of clearly defined ministry tasks to qualified workers, than working overtime and alone. Learning to trust others and their gifts and keeping those so entrusted to an accountable plan will build up the kingdom of God and strengthen the overall work of the church. Of all the resources available to reduce stress and burnout in ministers, delegation of responsibilities to others is clearly one of the most important and often under-utilized tools of leadership management. Again, willingness to work, a good attitude, and a teachable servant-heart are qualities that shine even above one's natural talents or ability to perform. Many a delegated responsibility has been accomplished with glowing reports due to a cooperative spirit and a Christ-like attitude. Pastors are reluctant, and rightly so, to use people whose hearts and attitudes are not in unity with the purposes of the church.

10 – Demands and Expectations

Even gifted and able people may oftentimes not be used because of lingering attitudes and issues of the heart. To delegate to this type of person can cause disaster. Leaders need to know their people, as a shepherd knows his sheep. There are new leaders waiting to be discovered in the midst of any congregation. It is the wise pastor who goes looking for trustworthy people to whom God can entrust responsibility and authority to share in ministry life.

When Conflict Comes

Ministers face conflict at a variety of levels. When conflict from within a church occurs, it can be most difficult to handle, as a leader usually has high expectations of believers and staff volunteers under his leadership. The emotional pain and sense of loss are very real and affect clergy, volunteers, and the individuals in that particular ministry program. Conflicts create a tension and stress level in congregations and an awareness of individuals in need of effective and loving attention. Misunderstandings over the direction of a church, or the agenda of a pastor, can easily develop into an unhealthy conflict. Ministers have reported that it is conflict over personality differences, methods of management, or misunderstandings that have created stress and tension.

The Lord has given authority to the pastor, but that authority must also be respected by the congregation and used in appropriate ways. With a servant's heart, the leader can create a healing atmosphere where truth is expressed in a loving and grace-giving environment. Humbleness and a genuine desire to see health restored should guide the pastor during times of conflict. Congregations often need more information, better communication, and the assurance that their leaders are men and women who want the best for the body of Christ. There will always be those that are antagonistic to leadership and authority, and those individuals need special prayer, and at times appropriate confrontation, to address the attitudes of the heart. Haugk (1988), in his book *Antagonists in the Church*, does a superb job of defining the personality of antagonists and the ways leaders should handle these manipulative, often explosive, and painful individuals.

Conflict and crisis should be seen as opportunities where the leader learns to trust the Lord alone for wisdom and grace. These

Finishing Well

negative experiences should be seen as teaching tools of the Lord for the maturing that will assist others. Paul said, " Praise be to God and the Father of our Lord Jesus Christ, the Father of compassion and the God of all comfort, who comforts us in all our troubles, so that we can comfort those in any trouble with the comfort we ourselves have received from God" (2 Cor.1:3-4). It was in the crises of life that Paul says he learned the comfort of God. In turn, Paul was able to comfort and assist others in their own trials and troubles. The maturing gained in conflicted relationships and crisis situations affects both the spiritual and ministerial formation of ministers (Clinton, 1988, p. 159). Paul saw the hard times in his own life as a source of encouragement, as God enabled, was present, and was sufficient for all his needs. Conflict and crisis can be used by God to instruct us in His ultimate purposes, and to develop a deeper relationship with Christ Himself. Many ministers fail at this point to understand the good that can come out of bad situations. They often become bitter and calloused, and remain blocked from further growth and maturity. Many resign from ministry during the hard times of their experience, rather than learning from them and moving on in their walk and leadership development. Learning to be positive in a negative situation is a true mark of spiritual maturity.

In answer to specific prayers, a leader can see the hand of God even in the hard times. The New Testament shows us the response of leaders in the midst of a crisis. James 1:2-4; Second Corinthians 1:3-4; and Second Timothy 3:10-11, all reveal the way leadership ministered in the midst of great difficulties and crises. The expectation of congregations is that their minister has all the answers and can manage nearly every possible situation with grace and wisdom. Such an expectation on a pastor can create stress and anxiety. What the minister needs to know is that God has placed them at this critical time in a church or a family situation, so that He might work through them for His glory and for His purposes.

Ministers are not the 'answer men', who always have the right thing to say or respond correctly every time there is an emergency or crisis. That should be one's goal - to be an instrument in the hands of God - but the reality recognizes one's limitations and human weakness. Doing one's best, and leaving the results to God, would be

10 – Demands and Expectations

a fair principle by which to live. Healthy ministers remember that it is God who gives the increase.

Living with Losses

The high demands and expectations of congregants also include the area of loss. Dr. Archibald Hart, in speaking on the issues of finishing well, shared the concept that ministry is a vocation of loss. Dr. Hart said that ministers need to learn to accept losses so as to better deal with the depression that may come through emotional drain, physical strain, and spiritual loss. People move, have a variety of ways of relating, and identify with certain personalities, so much so, that the minister is in the middle of a lot of opportunities for loss. There is the loss of leadership, loss of families, death of members, and the constantly changing patterns of urban unrest. It is the everyday erosion in relationships that causes caregivers added stress. It is a hard calling to be a people-person, and it takes skill, competence, and ability to handle the variety of issues that require ministering in love and grace to a community of believers. Not all people can handle the losses that are part and parcel of ministry leadership equally well. The solution is to develop support systems which would include strong spiritual disciplines and accountability groups who love and care for the caregiver.

Depression may come and must be dealt with for health and vitality to be restored to the caregiver. Self-care, as described by H.B. London in a chapter entitled 'Eight Ways to Grow a Great Soul' (*The Heart of a Great Pastor*, 1994, p. 186-194), reminds us to be pro-active and continually before the Lord, open to His instruction.

Training in Conflict Resolution

Ministry leaders face the test of their authority and relational skills when they are in the middle of dealing with conflict. There are sufficient tools and materials on the market to assist leaders in developing conflict management skills. *Peacemakers*, developed and led by Ken Sande, is one such resource that systematically takes one through the scriptures and gives clear direction and clarification of what approach to take at specific levels of conflict. Training of one's

Finishing Well

church leadership team in this area will help in preparing people to understand and resolve church conflicts, as well as interpersonal conflicts.

Church life is all about relationships with people - each unique, and each a needy person. Christ has given the church gifts, individuals, and resources that include His Spirit, His Word, and capable individuals who are led by the Spirit to minister during the hard times. Transformation of individuals takes place when there is a willingness to follow the direction of the Lord and to be obedient in sharing the gospel to those in need.

Summary

There will always be demands and expectations of ministry leaders, and there will always be conflicts. Clergy should develop a habit of being realists; examining their motives; and reflecting on their own job descriptions. Talking to people openly about the direction of the church and its ministries will help ensure a team spirit. Maintaining balance in the use of time, and knowing one's limits, will bring spiritual and physical health. Reviewing priorities of ministry and congregational needs will keep the church and pastor on track.

Ministry is finding solutions to everyday circumstances and relationships. It is leaning on Jesus and not our own understanding. It is rising up in courage to remind people of God's standard, His help, and His power to transform our broken and often dysfunctional lives. Only as ministers take the role of servant-leader, following in the footsteps of Christ, and bringing people to the place of surrender, discipleship, and maturity, will the church be strong and make a difference in the world. Christ proclaimed, "I will build My church and the gates of hell will not prevail against it!" (Matt. 16:18) It is His church, His people, and we trust that He will manifest His power through the ministers and the flock for which He gave Himself at Calvary.

10 – Demands and Expectations

Discussion and Action Steps dealing with

DEMANDS AND EXPECTATIONS

Investigative Questions to Consider

1. Who sets your schedule of activities - the church or you?

2. Do you have a written job description? Is it followed or reviewed?

3. Does your church body know what your schedule is, office hours, time off?

4. Do you have a reasonable view of what ministry involves? Does your spouse?

5. Are you able to get adequate rest and recreation to stay healthy?

6. How do you respond to emergencies; crisis situations?

7. When you delegate ministry assignments, are you able to trust those people?

8. What do you do really well? What is a weakness for you in ministry?

9. Do you feel 'called' to minister in your present situation?

10. What is your primary focus at this time? Is it growing pains as a church body, broken relationships, stress from high personal expectations?

11. What are you doing to alleviate stress and burnout in ministry?

12. Do you have any personal issues of the past that need resolution?

Finishing Well

13. Are you competitive in spirit? If so, what is driving that factor?

Action Steps

1. Write out a job description and share it with your spouse and church board.

2. Do an in-depth study of Jesus in the area of his 'pace of activities'.

3. If you are a driven person, find ways of rest and renewal in God.

4. Establish limits on your time, involvement, and appointments so as to safeguard your private life.

5. Join a gym or fitness club and make it a practice to keep in shape.

6. Do a daily time audit to evaluate your ministry time and priorities.

7. Attend a course on Conflict Resolution skills training.

CHAPTER 11

YOU CAN FINISH WELL!

A Strong Start in the Calling of God

Finishing well is dependent on many things that a person does or believes. It has as much to do with attitude as with one's actions and habits. For a man or woman of God to finish well, they must have a clear understanding of a strong start based on the holy calling of God to a ministry life. Leaders are in a God-given position to influence and to impact, not to impress the community and families around them. First Peter 4:10 : "Each one should use whatever gift he has received to serve others, faithfully administering God's grace in its various forms." Recognition of the touch of God upon a servant of the church affirms that individual to the ministry of Christ for building up the body for works of service.

We identified the general call to ministry as one that is extended to the whole body of Christ. Every Christian is to participate in doing ministry within the area of one's gifts and abilities. The special call of God to those whom God would use as leaders in His Church is a specific and definable calling. The Lord chooses some to be pastors and leaders for the benefit of others. It is a holy calling and one in which God equips, trains, and develops over a lifetime. Those so set apart for a shepherding role are identified in scripture and recognized by the church as spiritual leaders.

Discovering the Stressors of Ministry

The various ministry surveys and publications all indicate that stress and burnout happen to pastors and leadership irregardless of denomination or personality differences. Everyone experiences stress in life, but it is the caregivers who seem to have additional stress due to a variety of reasons. We discovered that there are many things that contribute to clergy stress, many of which can be managed for more effective and healthier lives. The five major stressors were identified as differences in the style of leadership, time management, accountability, nurturing relationships, and demands and expectations resulting in conflicted relationships. Each of these areas can be managed so that the pastor can strengthen their skills, and work within the strengths of their ministry gifts.

Faith is tested on the mountaintop, as Abraham learned when he took Isaac as a sacrifice. Leadership is tested, as everyone's life will at some time be tested (MacDonald, 2000). The work of ministry brings with it the great resources of God to meet the ever-increasing demands and expectations of the congregation. The joy of seeing people come to Christ and grow in love and holiness draws many to consider the profession and calling of pastor. To be effective, we need to be genuine people, in what Hands and Fehr (1993) conclude by stating that "to move toward real intimacy with self, others, and God, I must begin by facing the reality of my life" (p. 74).

Ministers are a part of the human race and need to acknowledge their own limits and rely on the grace and goodness of God to forgive, call, and empower. True health for clergy is an integrated viewpoint of our humanity with the understanding that we are healed healers, saved sinners reaching out to others in need of the Savior's love and grace. Finishing well includes balancing one's time and relationships, recognizing our physical needs and limits, and understanding the biblical expectations made upon us in ministry.

Developing Governing Principles for Finishing Well

Governing principles to stay healthy in the calling of minister give us safeguards by which to live. One's character, commitment, and competency are foundational aspects of our personhood. They are what determine in large part how God will use us in sharing His ministry with others. We need to know ourselves, our personality, our gifts, our styles of relating, and how God has wired us, before we can effectively minister to others. Ministry for a lifetime means we see the journey as a marathon and not a sprint.

One of the ongoing tasks of pastors should be in the area of leadership development. Learning how to be an effective leader, and how to apply one's skills to given tasks, will strengthen what God has already given. Good leaders are those who are lifelong learners - willing to listen, think, and grow by investing in themselves.

11 – You Can Finish Well

God did not call people to ministry to have them burn out, or to quit. God has given all that we need for life and godliness in Christ Jesus. The problem seems to be in our understanding or in the outworking of that call and our independence from God to accomplish His plans. We are reminded that it is the work of the Lord we are in; it is not our work, nor is it our harvest. The church and its entire people, the world, and all the needs represented there truly belong to the Lord. "Unless the Lord builds the house, they labor in vain that build it" (Ps. 127:1, KJV). Fuller Theological Seminary professor, Dr. Archibald Hart, quoted a study by Bob Buford, from a book *"Finishing Well: What People Who Really Live Do Differently" (2005),* that only 1 in 4 professionals and leaders finish well. The remainder bottom out, drop out, or are let go from their responsibilities. God would have it otherwise.

We see a great principle of the source of our strength in Second Corinthians 4:7-9 : "We have this treasure in jars of clay to show that this all-surpassing power is from God and not from us. We are hard pressed on every side, but not crushed; perplexed, but not in despair; struck down, but not destroyed." It is Christ in us - not ourselves, not our gifts, not our education or experience - that builds the kingdom. Making a strong finish in ministry requires us to start on the right path, in the call of God. Then through the course of the leading of the Lord in the journey, we find ourselves being equipped and strengthened by maintaining the spiritual disciplines and also making ourselves accountable to others. The issues are many and vary from person to person, but the main theme is to know the Lord, know yourself, and know where to go for help when the need arises. Ministry is more than doing things for the Lord and His people; it is being the person of integrity and honesty that will submit to the teachings of the Lord and follow His example in our lives.

In all of our discussion about leadership development, and the necessity to stay strong and healthy in the work, we come to the question: What does a godly leader look like? Clinton (1988, p. 74) believes "a godly leader is a person with God-given capacity and God-given responsibility to influence specific groups of God's people toward His purposes for the group." Defining a leader in Christian ministry is quite different than comparing with a business or secular model of leadership. Some of the same qualities and values do

Finishing Well

overlap, but in the end, it is the Bible that gives us the characteristics of a godly man or woman. The world's way of evaluating may be by production quotas, influence, or value based on achievement or size. Scripture teaches us that faithfulness is far more valued by God than size of organization, influence, or income. Finishing well means we use our gifts and abilities, with a commitment to the call of God, to accomplish His plans and purposes for the people we have been given to shepherd. Again, we are responsible to people, to carry out effective and faith-based ministry, but not for their responses or choices.

Problems and conflicted relationships are an area of great stress. Role conflict and feelings of futility suggest a lack of understanding one's calling, or how one relates their gifts and abilities to their ministerial function. Each of these stressors, as well as the variety of events and issues that may affect an individual, are all reasons to clarify one's calling and role, and to understand themselves, their gifts, and their limitations.

Developing a balanced life and ministry takes time and effort on the part of each of us. The Lord has given all that we need for life and godliness. In the special calling to pastoral ministry, God has provided the strength, wisdom, and opportunities for support to not only establish an effective ministry, but also to sustain it. By practicing discipline in the areas of spiritual health as a foundational basis from which to grow one's ministry, the Lord can then build on that firm foundation of character, competency, and commitment.

As we noted in Chapter 5, there are areas of professional ministry life that need our attention and effort. The challenges of ministry will be different for each individual, and each individual's calling and situation, but the perceptive and receptive minister will realize the areas of their lives that need reinforcement and ongoing improvement. When there are supportive people and times of Sabbath rest and renewal for the minister, there is a better chance for longevity of ministry.

With an open heart, and a commitment to excellence, leadership can gain insight and improve with the help of the Lord and a variety of support systems. Today there are a host of organizations and ministries that exist solely for the purpose of strengthening ministers and their families. Retention of ministers for the long haul

11 – You Can Finish Well

requires church boards and ministers themselves to pay attention to signs of stress and the health of the minister and his family. Finishing well in ministry, and life in general, is ultimately an integrity issue. Will we maintain personal spiritual and moral disciplines in the midst of our calling? Will ministers submit to the clear teaching of Scripture and live out the gospel of Jesus Christ? It appears to this author that the other issues of leadership style, use of time, and so on, are all based on the essential foundation stones of character, competency, and commitment. It is who we are in private and in public - our very personhood, which is the 'living epistle known and read by men' - that gets the job done.

Finishing well in the eyes of God is more than having a successful ministry, church facility, or following. It is obedience to the Lordship of Christ. It is sacrificial giving and living. It is washing feet with a servant's heart. It is not ambition, self-confidence, talents, or charisma, but that quiet, steady, faithfulness to the calling of Christ.

God is more concerned about who we are than what we do. The will of God has more to do with being a servant of Christ, than being in a position of authority or leadership. Fulfilling the plan of God is essentially living out the inner qualities of Christ in one's public life and less to do with achievement. Success by the standard of the Gospel is hearing the words of Christ, "Well done, thou good and faithful servant". (Matt. 25:21)

By maintaining the principles that affect our character, develop our competency, help us keep our commitment, and build on the call of God, we can then manage, motivate, and succeed in the face of trials, setbacks, and crises. Standing upon the basics, which are often forgotten in the busyness of life, will ensure that we not only finish the tasks for which we were called, but finish well. In good health, spiritual grace, and joy, the servant of the Lord can see the hand of God leading, guiding, and providing for all they need. We have many helps and tools to understand and use to finish well the life and ministry which God has given. May we choose wisely and maintain our lives in Christian faith, fulfilling the call of God in spiritual health.

Like Paul the Apostle, ministers can say, "I have fought the good fight; I have finished the race; I have kept the faith" (2 Tim.4:7). With the resources of the Lord, men and women in ministry can

Finishing Well

continue in His strength, as the Holy Spirit spoke through Paul: "Being confident of this, that He who began a good work in you will carry it on to completion until the day of Christ Jesus" (Phil. 1:6). We, too, are to press on to take hold of that for which Christ Jesus took hold of us, even pressing on to the goal to win the prize for which God has called us heavenward in Christ Jesus (Phil. 3:12,14).

May you start well, minister in health,

and

"finish well"!

*"But none of these things move me, neither count I my life dear unto myself, so that **I might finish my course with JOY**, and the ministry, which I have received of the Lord Jesus, to testify the gospel of the grace of God."* (Acts 20:24, KJV)

APPENDIX A
STRESS SYMPTOMS

The following came from researcher Dr. Hans Selye, endocrinologist at McGill University, 1930's. Inlander, Charles B., and Moran, Cynthia K. *Stress; 63 Ways to Relieve Tension and Stay Healthy.* New York City, NY: Walker and Company, 1996.

Behavioral/Emotional

Anger and hostility
Apprehension
Blaming others
Complaining
Critical of self & others
Crying
Defensive Behavior
Denial
Depression
Diminished initiative
Excessive alcohol use
Excessive smoking
Gulping meals
Habitual teeth grinding
   (bruxism)
Indecisiveness
Irritability
Lack of satisfaction
   from happy experiences
Mistrust
Mood Swings
Nail Biting
Panic
Restlessness
Suicidal tendencies
Withdrawal

Intellectual

Diminished fantasy life
Forgetfulness
Lack of attention to detail
Lack of awareness of
   external stimuli
Lack of concentration
Past rather than future
   orientation
Preoccupation
Reduced creativity

Physical

Anorexia
Chronic fatigue
Constipation
Cool, clammy skin
Diarrhea
Dilated pupils
Disturbed motor skills
Dry mouth
Frequent urination
Headaches
Heart palpitations
Hyperactivity
Hyperventilation
Impaired Sexual Dysfunction
Insomnia
Itchy scalp
Loss of appetite
Nausea and/or vomiting
Over-eating
Rash
Sneezing
Spasm of the hands and feet
Stooped posture
Sweaty palms
Tight muscles
Trembling, tics; Indigestion, stomachaches

Finishing Well

APPENDIX B

WOLYNIAK SURVEY RESULTS

Survey was sent to 30 ministers. There were 16 responses. August 15, 2004. Rating was 5 for agree; 1 for disagree. Results are in percent.

A. Personal Life Relationship with the Lord.

1. What I believe about God has changed in the last few years.

5	4	3	2	1
6%	6	6	31	50

2. I find new discoveries from the Bible in my daily devotions.

5	4	3	2	1
31	63	6	-	-

3. I am committed to living a life of holiness and am diligent in pursuing godliness.

5	4	3	2	1
56	38	6	-	-

4. My personal walk with God is more important than my public walk in ministry.

5	4	3	2	1
63	31	6	-	-

5. I am growing in new areas of discipline and growth.

5	4	3	2	1
31	50	6	6	-

6. I am hungry and eager to see God touch the key areas of my life with His Spirit.

5	4	3	2	1
69	25	6	-	-

7. I feel that my life is a holy life that pleases God, who sees in secret.

5	4	3	2	1
12	38	44	6	-

8. I should pray more.

5	4	3	2	1
44	44	12	-	-

Appendix B- Wolyniak Survey Results

9. I wish I could take a sabbatical - a few months away from ministry, for renewal.

5	4	3	2	1
38	44	-	12	6

10. I feel healthy spiritually and am in good shape.

5	4	3	2	1
12	38	44	6	-

B. Family and spouse relationships; shared goals; objectives for the family.

1. My spouse shares the same enthusiasm for ministry and outreach.

5	4	3	2	1
38	50	12	-	-

2. I have shared time devotionally and in prayer with my spouse.

5	4	3	2	1
31	12	12	31	12

3. My family comes first after my relationship with God.

5	4	3	2	1
63	31	6	-	-

4. I am able to structure my time to best benefit my family.

5	4	3	2	1
25	50	12	6	-

5. I view the ministry I have as a team effort that includes my spouse and family.

5	4	3	2	1
44	38	12	6	-

6. My spouse is supportive of my time at the office and with church families.

5	4	3	2	1
50	44	6	-	-

7. I have regular times of recreation and rest with my family on a monthly basis.

5	4	3	2	1
19	38	38	6	-

8. My children are appreciative of the ministry work that I do.

5	4	3	2	1
31	50	6	6	-

Finishing Well

9. I am fulfilling the primary goals I have for my family and spouse.

5	4	3	2	1
19	50	25	6	-

10. My spouse is my best friend.

5	4	3	2	1
63	25	12	-	-

C. Preparation for ministry: training, gifts, experience.

1. I attended a Bible school that gave adequate training in human relations.

5	4	3	2	1
-	19	38	31	12

2. My theological education prepared me for the conflicts in ministry.

5	4	3	2	1
-	6	31	44	19

3. The gifts I have received from God are currently being used to their fullest.

5	4	3	2	1
-	63	25	12	-

4. I handle stress in ministry very well.

5	4	3	2	1
6	25	44	25	-

5. I have a strong sense of call to be a pastor.

5	4	3	2	1
75	19	6	-	-

6. I am always reading and looking for new insights to assist in ministry efforts.

5	4	3	2	1
19	69	6	6	-

7. Preaching and teaching are my strong points.

5	4	3	2	1
38	44	19	-	-

8. Pastoral care and discipleship are where I like to spend my time.

5	4	3	2	1
12	50	31	6	-

9. People have told me that my ministry is appreciated.

5	4	3	2	1
44	44	6	6	-

Appendix B- Wolyniak Survey Results

10. The confirmation of the call of God to ministry is readily apparent to all.

5	4	3	2	1
56	44	-	-	-

11. It is difficult for me to motivate people in the congregation.

5	4	3	2	1
6	38	31	19	6

12. Interpersonal conflict never really taxes me.

5	4	3	2	1
6	12	12	44	25

13. I would rather preach than do administrative tasks.

5	4	3	2	1
31	38	25	6	-

14. Meeting people's needs is a task I truly enjoy.

5	4	3	2	1
31	25	38	6	-

15. Administration and leadership skills are my strong points.

5	4	3	2	1
6	31	44	19	-

16. I had adequate training in conflict resolution and management.

5	4	3	2	1
-	6	25	44	25

17. I am very satisfied with my present role as a minister.

5	4	3	2	1
12	56	19	12	-

18. My church and I are a good match.

5	4	3	2	1
31	50	19	-	-

D. Ongoing healthy relationships of peers in ministry.

1. I have several close friends in ministry to whom I make myself accountable.

5	4	3	2	1
6	38	25	6	25

2. My district and sectional leaders are open to me and supportive of my ministry.

5	4	3	2	1
50	25	19	6	-

Finishing Well

3. If I was struggling in an area of my life, I would freely go to one of my leaders.

5	4	3	2	1
19	25	25	25	6

4. I take criticism, correction, or rebuke very well.

5	4	3	2	1
-	50	19	25	-

5. I try to establish lasting relationships with new ministers in our area.

5	4	3	2	1
12	19	25	31	12

6. I feel that I am on a team of ministers fulfilling the Great Commission.

5	4	3	2	1
31	38	19	12	-

7. I do not feel that I am in competition with others in ministry.

5	4	3	2	1
50	38	12	-	-

8. I do not feel lonely in life or ministry at this time.

5	4	3	2	1
38	25	19	19	-

9. If I was struggling in an area of my life, I would keep to myself and trust God.

5	4	3	2	1
19	19	31	31	-

10. If my peers really knew me, they would like what they found in me.

5	4	3	2	1
25	56	19	-	-

11. I have people to turn to when struggling, but I most likely will not do so.

5	4	3	2	1
12	38	19	25	6

E. Core values and experiences that are unique to the person: past history, family of origin; attitudes to authority.

1. Honesty and integrity are very important to me.

5	4	3	2	1
94	6	-	-	-

Appendix B- Wolyniak Survey Results

2. Submitting to authority has always been easy.

5	4	3	2	1
31	38	25	6	-

3. I am humbled to be allowed by God to be in a position of leadership.

5	4	3	2	1
88	12	-	-	-

4. I can preach and teach as good as anyone in my fellowship.

5	4	3	2	1
-	25	38	31	-

5. I believe that a person can preach and teach without the help of the Lord.

5	4	3	2	1
-	-	12	38	50

6. I want to be seen as one who has done well in life and ministry.

5	4	3	2	1
63	31	6	-	-

7. Time is more important to me than money and success.

5	4	3	2	1
31	31	38	-	-

8. I have a conflict with my superiors that is unresolveable.

5	4	3	2	1
-	-	6	12	81

9. The truth of God is more important than protecting relationships.

5	4	3	2	1
31	38	25	-	-

10. I like to be around people who are much different than I am.

5	4	3	2	1
12	25	44	19	-

11. I prefer to be around people who are just like me theologically and spiritually.

5	4	3	2	1
-	25	44	25	6

12. My parents raised me to know the Lord, and lived the life of Christ openly.

5	4	3	2	1
50	25	-	-	25

Finishing Well

13. Man is basically good and just needs the Lord to bring out the best in them.

5	4	3	2	1
-	6	12	19	63

14. Success to me is being faithful to the task to which God has called me.

5	4	3	2	1
81	19	-	-	-

15. I believe I have discovered my spiritual gifts for ministry.

5	4	3	2	1
56	38	6	-	-

16. People are more important than my plans and day-timer.

5	4	3	2	1
63	31	6	-	-

APPENDIX C

Wolyniak Survey-General Question Results

The following results are from the Wolyniak Survey. They are the background questions. These were general questions on a separate page. There were 16 pastors responding.

1. How many years have you pastored? (24.56 years ave.)

0-4 yrs	5-8 yrs.	9-12 yrs	13-16 yrs	17-20 yrs	21 plus
-	6%	-	12%	12%	69%

2. How many years have you pastored your current church? (10.81 years ave.)

0-3	4-6	7-9	10-12	13-15	16 +
-	25%	19%	38%	-	19%

3. How many churches have you pastored, or served as an associate? (3.62 churches)

1	2	3	4	5	6	7	8
12%	12	25	25	12	6	-	6

4. Do you work outside the church?   YES 6%; NO= 94%

5. What is your highest level of formal education?

HS	BS	MA	DMin	Other
12%	63	25	-	-

6. Did you graduate from Bible College?   YES= 81%; NO= 19%

7. Did you graduate from Seminary?   YES= 19%; NO= 81%

8. Have you ever experienced a forced exit? YES= 19%; NO= 81%

9. How old were you when you first considered becoming a pastor?

12-17 yrs	18-25	26-35	36+
56%	31%	12%	zero

10. Have you ever received a sabbatical while in ministry? YES= 25%; NO= 75%

Finishing Well

APPENDIX D

THE PURPOSE OF THE MENTORING PROGRAM

The Rocky Mountain District Council has established the Mentoring Program to assist our pastors and ministers to be more effective servants of the Lord in their specific areas of ministry. As a requirement for Ordination, the Mentoring Program is designed to facilitate more contact with our candidates and to assist them in several areas. The Presbytery desires to encourage, strengthen, and clarify the calling of men and women to Christian ministry. The following descriptions may serve to assist in defining the overall purpose of the Mentoring Program with our potential Ordination Candidates with the Assemblies of God.

MINISTRY ISSUES THAT NEED TO BE ADDRESSED

The Mentoring Program was designed to address some of the following ministry issues that have occurred in the past years in our district.

1. The lack of a clear understanding of the "call of God" to ministry. Some have seen ministry as a profession rather than a call of God.

2. Pastoral burnout due to a lack of understanding of the demands of the pastorate, and the expectations of ministers of what ministry will be like.

3. A lack of understanding of the relationship issues that hinder the effectiveness of ministry. Personality type and general people skills often are in need of clarification.

4. Personal failures that affect pastoral and ministerial care. These would include financial, sexual, and leadership issues. Family life and the minister's marriage are of vital importance to a healthy and rewarding ministry.

Appendix D - Mentoring Program

THE PURPOSE OF THE MENTORING PROGRAM DEFINED

1. By assigning a mentor to a candidate, we establish an ***accountability*** system to ensure that the candidate accomplishes the items that need to be addressed. The Candidate will sign a contractual agreement with the Mentor, who in turn will have a final evaluation form to present to the Presbytery for their review.

2. The Candidate and mentor *meet on a regular basis*, normally monthly, to speak to the following issues. Times of discussion and discovery about the following basic issues as well as other issues personal to the individual minister.

    a. Position paper published by the Assemblies of God entitled, "Theological and Functional Dimensions of Ordination".
    b. Discuss and discover how to protect oneself from pastoral stressors and potential burnout.
    c. Discuss how the candidate is handling the issues of the "Deadly Sins for Church Leaders Today". (Handout provided from Leadership Journal, Spring 2001).
    d. Discuss the handout: "The Seven Deadly Sins". (Leadership Journal, Spring 2001).
    e. Discuss and investigate the seven areas listed in the "Proposed Guidelines for Mentors" handout.

3. The Mentor/Candidate relationship is designed to assist the Candidate to *understand the dynamics of ministry* through discussions, readings, inquiry, and research on the above stated topics. This is a wonderful opportunity to address areas that may need improvement, such as the minister's character, skills, competence, or commitment. The Mentor gives guidance, encouragement, and wisdom from their personal life experiences.

Finishing Well

4. The Mentoring Program is established to ensure that the Ordination Candidate has *addressed both the professional and personal expectations and qualifications* of ministry as an Assemblies of God minister. Many of those in ministry have accomplished a fine academic record, but may lack personal skills or are unaware of the stressors and demands of ministry life today. The mentor is in a position to address those blind spots and give guidance and assistance to the Candidate.

5. The Mentoring Program is designed to foster a *deep friendship* in a trusting environment whereby the Candidate can be open and candid in their responses to discussion topics. As all in ministry have times of great hardship, as well as great joys and dreams, the mentor has the opportunity to speak into the candidate's life.

6. The Mentoring Program can help to *integrate the lessons of life as a Biblicist* in daily ministry routines. There is a need to discover what the Bible has to say on specific issues the minister may be facing. As culture changes, there are more opportunities for the minister to share the foundational truths of the gospel. The maturing process in ministry takes place at both the personal level as well as the public relationship dynamics level. The mentor, having been in ministry for a longer period of time, has a larger reservoir of life experiences and perhaps a better understanding of those dynamics that the minister will have to deal with in the pastorate.

7. A final purpose is to *develop a healthy pattern of thinking and living* that will outlive the mentoring relationship. By establishing a spirit of critical thinking, honest evaluation, and planned accountability, the mentoring program can strengthen the minister's life for the long haul. The mentoring process can direct the candidate to principles and resources that have the potential to keep the calling of God alive and strong for a lifetime of ministry. The topic of balance in life is of vital importance and should be the final outcome of the mentoring program. The demands of ministry are very great today, and if

Appendix D - Mentoring Program

ministers are to do more than survive - to thrive - then they must establish themselves in the Lord on a personal level, as well as in the context of accountable relationships with peers and those in an advisory capacity.

Summary:

The Mentoring Program has as its primary goal the concept of helping younger ministers clarify their calling and routinely evaluate their attitudes, motives, and heart for ministry. It also is a tool to help bring an awareness and ownership of the tremendous privilege and responsibility that comes with ordination into full-time ministry.

Ministers, as never before, need the help, advice, friendship, and relationships of others who have served as servants of Christ Jesus. The mentoring program can bolster, challenge, and assist to keep accountable those ministers so as to ensure the continuing health and vigor of ministry for the greater good of the kingdom of God. The Bible says that in the multitude of counselors there is safety, and such is the desire of the mentoring program. It is the desire of the Rocky Mountain District to keep its ministers safe and strong, the ministry ever expanding and growing, and the principles of Christian living presented to its church congregations through living examples of the grace and love of Jesus Christ.

==

NOTE: The above document is now a part of the process for working with Ordination Candidates. Submitted by Dale Wolyniak.

Finishing Well

APPENDIX E

INTERNET RESOURCES

LEADERSHIP

www.alban.org	Alban Institute
www.comd.org	Center for Organizational Ministry Development.
www.christianitytoday.com	Christianity Today
www.breakoutofthebox.com	Ennegram Leadership Styles (nine)
www.odysseycoaching.com	Executive coaching
http://psychology.about.com	Leadership Assessment Tools
http://www.cba.uri.edu	Leadership Style (Richard W. Scholl)
http://www.leadershipq.com	Leadership Test
www.leadershiptransformation.org	Leadership Transformation
www.mentorlink.gospel.com.net	Mentoring
http://www.myersbriggs.org	Myers-Briggs Type Indicator
http://www.casaa-resources.net	CASAA; Leadership styles
http://www.knowyourtype.com	Myers-Briggs Type Indicator
www.summit.org	Summit Ministries
http://www.solhamm.org	Style of Leadership (Manfred Davidmann)

LEGAL

www.alliancedefensefund.org	Alliance Defense Fund
www.christianlaw.org	Christian Law
www.churchlaw.org	Church Law Today
http://www.clergysupport.com/	Clergy Financial Services (tax issues)
www.rutherford.org	Rutherford Foundation

MARRIAGE & FAMILY

http://www.focusonthefamily.com	Focus on the Family
www.smalleyonline.com	Gary Smalley Ministries
www.ismk.com	International Society of Missionary Kids
www.justbetweenus.org	Just Between Us (wives)
www.mkassociation.com	Missionary Kids Association
www.mk.net	Missionary Kids
www.pastorswife.net	Pastor's Wife
www.pastorwives.org	Pastors' Wives
www.peacemaker.net	Peacemaker Ministries, Ken Sande
www.preacherskids.com	Preachers' Kids
www.shepherd-care.org	Shepherd Care
www.teenchallenge.com	Teen Challenge

Appendix E - Internet Resources

MINISTRY OPPORTUNITIES
www.christiannet.com	Christian Net
www.christianjobs.com	Christian Jobs
www.churchjobs.net	Church Jobs
www.churchstaff.com	Church Staff
www.churchstaffing.com	Church Staffing
www.flockfinder.com	Flock Finder
www.intercristosearchbase.com	Inter-Cristo
www.kingdomcareers.com	Kingdom Careers
www.ministryemployment.com	Ministry Employment
www.ministryjobs.com	Ministry Jobs
www.ministrylist.com	Ministry List
www.ministrysearch.com	Ministry Search
www.pastorsearch.net	Pastors' Search
www.youthspecialties.com	Youth Specialties
www.youthpastor.com	Youth Pastor

PASTORAL- sabbatical, compensation, articles
www.buildingchurchleaders.com	Building Church Leaders
www.clergyrenewal.org	Clergy Renewal
www.parsonage.org	Parsonage: Church and Clergy Department: Focus on the Family: Resources, referrals list
www.mtmfoundation.org	Sabbaticals
http://www.lillyendowment.org	Sabbatical funding help
www.troubledwith.com	Troubled With (articles on issues)

PERSONAL ISSUES; ADDICTIONS
www.covenanteyes.com	Covenant Eyes (Internet protection)
www.lovewonout.org	Love Won Out (help for sexual issues)
www.pureintimacy.org	Pure Intimacy (help for sexual issues)
www.purelifeministries.org	Pure Life Ministries (rehab)
www.stonegateresources.org	Stone Gate Resources (counseling)

REFERRAL COUNSELING
http://barnabas.org	Barnabas International
www.linkcare.org	Link Care Center
www.Parsonage.org	Focus on the Family: referrals for counseling, retreats.

RESEARCH
http://ag.org	Assemblies of God
http://www.barna.org	Barna Group
www.ctlibrary.com	Christianity Today Library
www.ellisonresearch.com	Ellison Research
www.equip.org	Equip
www.people-press.org	People Press

BIBLIOGRAPHY

Arndt, William F., and Gingrich, F. Wilbur. *A Greek-English Lexicon of the New Testament*. London: University of Chicago Press, Ltd., 1957, 16th printing.

Baab, Lynne M. *Beating Burnout in Congregations.* Bethesda, MD: Alban Institute, 2003.

Barna, George. *Leadership Journal*. Christianity Today International, Fall 2003, Vol. 24, No.4, p. 30.

_____. "A Profile of Protestant Pastors in Anticipation of Pastor Appreciation Month". *Leadership Journal*. Christianity Today, 25 September, 2001.

_____. *New Study Identifies the Strongest and Weakest Character Traits of Christian Leaders*. Barna Update. 2003. Database online. See www.barna.org.

_____. *Fish Out of Water: 9 Strategies Effective Leaders Use to Help You Get back Into the Flow*. Brentwood, TN: Integrity Publishing, 2002.

Barner, John, Pastoral Care Pastor, Focus on the Family. Interview by Dale Wolyniak, July 29, 2004, Colorado Springs, CO.

Batten, Joe, and Gail Batten, and Warren Howard. *The Leadership Principles of Jesus*. Joplin, MO: College Press, 1997.

Beckhard, Richard, and Marshall Goldsmith, and Frances Hesselbein, and Richard F.Schubert, ed. *The Future Series*. San Francisco, CA: Jossey-Bass Pub., 1998. The Drucker Foundation.

Biehl, Bobb. *Mentoring*. Nashville. TN: Broadman & Holman, 1996.

Finishing Well

Blanchard, Kenneth, and Bill Hybels, and Phil Hodges. *Leadership By the Book*. New York, NY: Water Brook Press, 1999.

Boers, Arthur P., 'Everyone's Pastor; No Ones Friend.' *Leadership*. IL: Christianity Today, Inc.: Winter 1991, Vol.12, No.1, p.130.

Bourke, Dale Hanson. *Turn Toward the Wind*. Grand Rapids, MI: Zondervan Publishing, 1995.

Bromiley, Geoffrey W. *Theological Dictionary of the New Testament*. Grand Rapids, MI: William B. Erdman's Publishing Company, 1985.

Brown, Collin ,ed. *The New International Dictionary of New Testament Theology*. Grand Rapids, MI: Regency Reference Library, 1975.

Bruce, Alexander Balman. *The Training of the Twelve*. Oak Harbor, WA: Logos Research Systems, Inc., 1995.

Brandt, Henry and Blackaby, Henry. *The Power of the Call*. Nashville, TN: Broadman & Holman, 1997.

Buchannan, Mark. *Your God is too Safe* . Sisters, OR: Multnomah Publishers, Inc., 2001.

Bullock, A. Richard, and Bruesehoff, Richard J. *Clergy Renewal*. The Alban Guide to   Sabbatical Planning, Bethesda, MD: Alban Institute, 2000.

Borthwick, Paul. *Leading the Way*. Colorado Springs, CO: Nav Press, 1989.

Buford, Bob. *Finishing Well: What Real People Who Really Live Do Differently!*. Brentwood, TN: Integrity Publishers, 2005

Bibliography

Carlson, Dwight. *Run and Not Be Weary*. Old Tappan, NJ: Fleming H. Revell Co., 1974.

Church Research Report, *The Work Week of A Pastor*. Christianity Today International, 1997 (by subscription only).

Clinton, J. Robert. *The Making of A Leader*. Colorado Springs, CO: Nav Press, 1988.

Clowney, Edmund P. *The Church*. Downers Grove, IL: Intervarsity Press, 1995.

Cooper, Rodney L. *Double Bind*. Grand Rapids, MI: Zondervan Publishing Co., 1996.

Crabb, Larry. *Shattered Dreams*. Colorado Springs, CO: Waterbrook Press, 2001.

Daniel, Stephen Paul. "Burn-Out and the Pastor, A Study on Stress in the Ministry." Doctor of Philosophy dissertation, Biola College, Inc., La Mirada, CA: 1981.

Dawn, Marva and Peterson, Eugene. *The Unnecessary Pastor*. Grand Rapids, MI: William B.Erdman's Publishing Co., 2000.

Demarco, Tom. *Slack*. New York City, NY: Broadway Books, 2001.

Donovan, Kathleen. *Growing Through Stress*. Berrien Springs, MI: Institute of World Mission, 2002.

Drucker, Peter F. *The Essential Drucker*. New York City, NY: Harper Collins Publishers, 2001.

Easton, M.G. *Easton's Bible Dictionary*. Oak Harbor, WA: Logos Research Systems, Inc., 1996.

Engstrom, Ted. *The Fine Art of Mentoring*. Brentwood, TN: Wolgemuth & Hyatt Publishing, Inc., 1989

Finishing Well

Enns, Paul. *The Moody Handbook of Theology.* Chicago, IL: Moody Press, 1996.

Exley, Richard. *Man of Character in a World of Compromise.* Tulsa, OK: Honor Books, 1995.

_____. *Perils of Power.* Hagerstown, MD: Review & Herald Graphics, 1995.

Farber, Barry A. *Stress and Burnout in the Human Service Professions.* Pergamon Press, 1983. (Pergamon General Psychology Series)

Farrar, Steve. *Finishing Strong.* Sisters, OR: Multnomah Publishers, 1995.

Faulkner, Brooks R. *Burnout In Ministry.* Nashville, TN: Broadman Press, 1981.

_____. *Stress in the Life of the Minister.* Nashville, TN: Convention Press, 1981

Fee, Gordon D. *The First Epistle to The Corinthians.* The New International Commentary on the New Testament. Grand Rapids, MI: William B. Erdman's Publishing Company, 1987.

Foyle, Marjory F. *Honorably Wounded.* Stress Among Christian Workers. Grand Rapids, MI: Monarch Books, 2001.

Gangel, Kenneth O. *Feeding and Leading.* Wheaton, IL: Victor Books, Scripture Press Publications, 1989.

George, Carl F., and Logan, Robert E. *Leading and Managing Your Church.* Old Tappan, NJ: Revell, 1987.

Gilbert, Barbara G. *Who Ministers to Ministers?.* Bethesda, MD: Alban Institute Pub., 1994.

Bibliography

Graham, Thomas. *Leadership Development: An Empowerment Model.* LaHabra, CA: COMD, 1998. Center for Organizational & Ministry Development.

Guiness, Os. *The Call.* Nashville, TN: Word Publishing Group, 1998.

_____. ed. *Character Counts.* Grand Rapids: Baker Books, 1999.

_____. *The Long Journey Home.* Colorado Springs, CO: Waterbrook Press, 2001.

Greenfield, Guy. *The Wounded Minister.* Grand Rapids, MI: Baker Books, 2001.

Hands, Donald R., and Fehr, Wayne L. *Spiritual Wholeness for Clergy.* Bethesda, MD: Alban Institute, 1993. (A new psychology of Intimacy with God, Self and Others)

Hansen, David. *The Art of Pastoring.* Downers Grove, IL: Intervarsity Press, 1994.

Hart, Archibald. Speech at a Pastor's Luncheon, Focus on the Family. Colorado Springs, CO: October, 2004.

Haugk, Kenneth C. *Antagonists In The Church.* Minneapolis, MN: Augsburg, 1988.

Headley, Anthony J. *Achieving Balance in Ministry.* Kansas City, KA: Beacon Hill Press, 1999.

Holoday, Margot, and Lackey, Trey, and Boucher, Michelle, and Glidewell, Reba. "Secondary Stress, Burnout, and the Clergy". *American Journal of Pastoral Counseling*, Vol. 4, (1). Haworth Press, 2001. Page 53-69.

Howard, J. Grant. *Balancing Life's Demands.* Portland, OR: Multnomah Books, 1977.

Finishing Well

Hulme, William Edward. *Managing Stress in Ministry.* San Francisco, CA: Harper and Row Publishers, 1982.

Inlander, Charles B. and Moran, Cynthia K. *Stress: 63 Ways to Relieve Tension and Stay Healthy.* New York City, NY: Walker Publishing Company, 1996.

Janz, Gregory. *Becoming Strong Again.* Grand Rapids, MI: Fleming H. Revell, 1998.

Jinkins, Michael, principal investigator , *Clergy Burnout Survey,* May 2002. Bethesada, MD, 2002. Austin Presbyterian Theological Seminary survey results published in *Congregations*, May/June 2002, by Alban Institute. Database available online by subscription to Alban Institute.

Jones, Kirk Byron. *Rest in the Storm.* Valley Forge, PA: Judson Press, 2001.

Keil, C.F., Delitzsch, F. *Commentary on the Old Testament.* Peabody: MA: Hendrickson Publishers, Inc., 2001. Vol. 1.

Kittel, Gerhard, and Friedrich, Gerhard, ed. *Theological Dictionary of the New Testament.* Grand Rapids, MI: William B. Erdman's Publishing Company, 1985.

Klauss, Allan C. "Great Expectations, Sobering Realities", *Congregations Journal.* Bethesda, MD: Alban Institute, 2002. May/June 2002, p.1-9.

Kollenberger III, John R., Goodrick, Edward W., and Swanson, James A. *The Greek English Concordance of the New Testament.* Grand Rapids, MI: Zondervan Publishing House, 1977.

LaHaye, Tim. *If Ministers Fall, Can they Be Restored.* Grand Rapids, MI: Pyranee Books, 1990.

Bibliography

Lloyd-Jones, D. Martyn. *Preaching and Preachers.* Grand Rapids, MI: Zondervan Publishing House, 1971.

Logan, Samuel T., ed. *The Preacher and Preaching.* NJ: P&R Publ.,1986.

London, H.B. *Pastors at Greater Risk.* Ventura, CA: Regal Books, 2003.

_____. *Refresh, Renew, Revive.* Colorado Springs, CO: Focus on the Family, 1996.

London, H.B., and Wiseman, Neil, B. *The Heart of A Great Pastor.* Ventura, CA: Regal Books, 1994.

_____. *They Call Me Pastor.* Ventura, CA: Regal Books, 2000.

_____. *Your Pastor is An Endangered Species.* Wheaton, IL: Victor Books, 1996.

Lucado, Max. *The Applause of Heaven.* Dallas, TX: Word Publishing, 1990.

Lucas, Jeff. Address given at 'Timberline Leadership Conference.' Fort Collins, CO: October 25-27, 2004.

Lutzer, Erwin W. *Pastor to Pastor.* Grand Rapids, MI: Kregel, 1998.

_____. *Seven Snares of the Enemy.* Chicago, IL: Moody Press, 2001.

Maslach, Christina. *Burnout-The Cost of Caring.* Englewood Cliffs, NJ: Prentice-Hall, Inc., 1982.

MacArthur, John, Jr. *Rediscovering Pastoral Ministry.* Nashville, TN: Word Publishing Group, 1995.

Finishing Well

MacDonald, Gordon. *Midcourse Correction.* Nashville, TN: Thomas Nelson Publishing, 2000.

Malphurs, Aubry. *Advanced Strategic Planning.* Grand Rapids, MI: Baker Books, 1999.

_____. *Ministry Nuts and Bolts.* Grand Rapids, MI: Kregel, 1997.

Matthews, R. Arthur. *Born For Battle.* New York, NY: Banta Company, 1988. An OMF publication.

Maxwell, John. *Developing the Leader Within You.* Nashville, TN: Thomas Nelson Publishers, 1993.

_____. *The 21 Indispensable Qualities of A Leader.* Nashville, TN: Thomas Nelson Publishers, 1993.

_____. TV interview with Joyce Meyers. PBS .October 5, 2004.

McGee, Robert S. *Father Hunger.* Ann Arbor, MI: Servant Publications, 1993.

McIntosh, Gary L. *One Size Doesn't Fit All.* Grand Rapids, MI: Fleming H. Revell, 1999.

McIntosh, Gary L., and Rima, Samuel D, Sr. *Overcoming the Dark Side of Leadership.* Grand Rapids, MI: Baker Books, 1997.

McKinley, Steve; and John Maxwell, and Greg Asimakoupoulos. *The Time Crunch.* Portland, OR: Multnomah Books, 1993.

Menzies, William. *Anointed to Serve.* Springfield, MO: Gospel Publishing House, 1971.

Meyer, Joyce. *A Leader in the Making.* Tulsa, OK: Harrison House, 2001.

Bibliography

Miller, Ardyce A. Director of Freedom Ministries. Interview by the Dale Wolyniak. November 21, 2000. Colorado Springs, Colorado.

Minirth, Frank, and Don Hawkins, and Paul Meier, and Richard Flournoy. *How to Beat Burnout*. Chicago, IL: Moody Bible Institute, 1986.

Moe, Kenneth Alan. *The Pastor's Survival Manual*. Bethesda, MD: Alban Institute, 1995.

Moore, Steve. *Leadership Insights*. Fort Worth, TX: Top Flight Leadership, 2002.

Moore, William J. "The Relationship Between Unrealistic Self-Expectations and Burnout Among Pastors." Ph. D. dissertation., Rosemead School of Psychology, La Mirada, CA: 1984.

New American Standard Bible, Copyright 1960, 1962, 1963, 1968, 1971, 1972,1973, 1975, 1977, by the Lockman Foundation.

O'Donnell, Kelly. *Doing Member Care Well*. Perspectives and Practices from Around the World. Pasadena, CA: World Evangelical Alliance Missions Commission, 2002.

Ortlund, Anne, and Ortlund, Ray. *Staying Power*. Nashville, TN: Oliver Nelson, 1989.

Oswald, Roy M. *Clergy Stress*. Bethesda, MD: Alban Institute, no date.

_____. *How to Build a Support System*. Bethesda, MD: Alban Institute, 1991.

Oswald, Roy M., and Kroeger, Otto. *Personality Type and Religious Leadership*. Bethesda, MD: Alban Institute, 1988.

Finishing Well

Pappas, Anthony G. *Pastoral Stress.* Bethesda, MD: Alban Institute, 1995.

Peterson, Eugene H. *Five Smooth Stones for Pastoral Work.* Grand Rapids, MI: William B. Erdman's Publishing Co., 1980.

_____. *The Contemplative Pastor.* Grand Rapids, MI: William B. Erdman's Publishing Co., 1989.

Pippert, Wesley. *The Hand of the Mighty.* Grand Rapids, MI: Baker Book House, 1991.

Randall, Robert L. *Walking Through the Valley.* (Understanding and Emerging from Clergy Depression), Nashville, TN: Abingdon Press, 1998.

Rassieur, Charles L. *Stress Management for Minister*s. Philadelphia, PA: Westminster Press, 1982.

Rediger, G. Lloyd. *Clergy Killers.* Louisville, KY: Westminster John Knox Press, 1997.

_____. *Coping With Clergy Burnout.* Valley Forge, PA: Judson Press, 1982.

Reed, Eric, and Hanson, Collin. "How Pastors Rate As Leaders." *Leadership Journal*, Fall 2003. (Christianity Today International. Church Research Report).

Ridderbos, Herman. *Paul, An Outline of His Theology.* Grand Rapids, MI: William B. Erdman's Publishing Co., 1975.

Roberts, Randall. *Lessons in Leadership.* Grand Rapids, MI: Kregel Publishers, 1999.

Rowell, Ed. *Leadership Journal*, Spring, 1998, Vol. 19, No.2, 1998, p. 86.

Bibliography

Rush, Myron. *Burnout*. Wheaton, IL: Victor Books, 1987.

Sanders, J. Oswald. *Paul the Leader*. Colorado Springs, CO: Nav Press, 1984.

Sanford, John A. *Ministry Burnout*. Louisville, KY: Westminster, John Knox Press, 1982. Paulist Press, NJ., 1982.

Schaper, Donna. *Common Sense About Men & Women In Ministry*. Bethesda, MD: Alban Institute, no date.

Seymor, Jody. *A Time for Healing*. Valley Forge: Judson Press, 1995.

Strait, C. Neil. *Pastor- Be Encouraged*. Kansas City, KA: Beacon Hill Press, 1996.

Stowell, Joseph M. *Shepherding the Church*. Chicago, IL: Moody Press, 1997.

Swanson, James. *Dictionary of Biblical Languages with Semantic Domains: Greek (New Testament)*. Oak Harbor, WA: Logos Research Systems, Inc., 1977.

Swenson, Richard A. *Margin*. Colorado Springs, CO: Nav Press, 1992.

Swindoll, Charles, R. *Dropping Your Guard*. Waco, TX: Word Books, 1983.

_____. *Flying Closer to the Flames*. Dallas, TX: Word Publishers, 1993.

_____. *Seasons of Life*. Portland, OR: Multnomah Press, 1983.

_____. *The Quest for Character*. Portland, OR: Multnomah Press, 1987.

Finishing Well

Sugden, Howard F., and Wiersbe, Warren W. *When Pastors Wonder How*. Chicago, IL: Moody, 1973, p. 9.

Tan, Siang-Yang, and Ortber, John Jr. *Understanding Depression*. Grand Rapids, MI: Baker Books, 1995

Taylor, William D., ed. *Too Valuable to Lose. Exploring the Causes and Cures of Missionary Attrition*. Pasadena, CA: William Carey Library, 1997.

Thayer, Joseph Henry. *A Greek English Lexicon of the New Testament*. New York, NY: Harper and Brothers, 1889.

The New Bible Dictionary. Wheaton, IL: Tyndale House Publishers, Inc., 1962.

The New International Version. *The Bible*. Nashville, TN: Broadman & Holman Publishers, 1996.

The Parsonage. August 25, 2001. "I See That Hand: What Do You See as Your Number One Priority". http://www.family.org/pastor/parsonpollarchive.cfm?&showresults=parsonage_0189.

Thomas, Clayton L., ed. *Taber's Cyclopedic Medical Dictionary*. Philadelphia, PA: F.A. Davis Company, 1985, 16th edition.

Turnbull, Ralph. *A Ministers Obstacles*. Grand Rapids, MI: Baker Book House, 1972.

Trask, Thomas E., and Womack, David A. *Back to the Altar*. Springfield, MO: Gospel Publishing House, 1995.

Trask, Thomas E., ed. *The Pentecostal Pastor*. Springfield, MO: Gospel Publishing House, 1997.

Bibliography

Walvoord, John F., and Zuck, Roy B. *The Bible Knowledge Commentary.* Wheaton, IL: Scripture Press Publications, Inc., 1985.

Wagner, E. Glenn. *Escape From Church, Inc.* Grand Rapids, MI: Zondervan, 1999.

Warren, Rick. *The Purpose Driven Life.* Grand Rapids, MI: Zondervan, 2002.

Weiser, Conrad W. *Healers-Harmed and Harmful.* Minneapolis, MN: Augsberg Fortress, 1994.

Wiersbe, Warren W. *The Integrity Crisis.* Nashville, TN: Oliver-Nelson Books, 1988.

_____. "Principles", *Leadership*, Winter, Volume I, No. 1, p. 81-88.

Wilkes, C. Gene. *Jesus on Leadership.* Wheaton, IL: Tyndale House Publishers, 1998.

Willard, Dallas. *Renovation of the Heart.* Colorado Springs, CO: Nav Press, 2002.

Willimon, William H. *Creative Leadership Series, Clergy and Laity Burnout.* Nashville, TN: Abington, 1989.

Woods, C. Jeff. *Better Than Success.* Valley Forge: Judson Press, 2001.

_____. *Congregational Megatrends.* Bethesda, MD: Alban Institute, 1996.

Zoba, Wendy Murray. *What Pastor's Wives Wish Churches Knew.* Leadership Journal. April 1997.